The Kent Ramblers

# The Tunbridge Wells Circular Walk

## and other walks in the Tunbridge Wells area

**ramblers**
at the heart of walking

Kent
**HIGH WEALD**
protect / explore / enjoy

EXPLOREKENT.ORG

**HIGH WEALD JOINT ADVISORY COMMITTEE**

**East Sussex**
County Council

ISBN: 978-1-906494-80-3

Published by Kent Ramblers
www.kentramblers.org.uk

Front cover: The Walks, Groombridge
This page: Eridge Park

# Contents

Introduction     4

Evolution of the Landscape     7

Tunbridge Wells Circular Walk:

    Part 1: Frant to Groombridge     10

    Part 2: Groombridge to Southborough     17

    Part 3: Southborough to Pembury     22

    Part 4: Pembury to Frant     28

    Link Route to Groombridge     32

    Link Route to Speldhurst     34

    Link Route from High Brooms     36

    Link Route to High Wood     37

Tunbridge Wells Heritage Walking Trail     38

Walks Through Time:

    Sissinghurst     49

    Benenden     55

    Goudhurst     62

    Bedgebury     68

    Cranbrook North     72

    Cranbrook South     74

A Brief History of the Weald     14

The Wealden Wool Industry     60

The Culpeper Family     61

The Cranbrook Colony     77

Decimus Burton     78

About the Ramblers     79

Acknowledgments     80

Waymarking and Signposting     81

4

# Introduction

## Tunbridge Wells Circular Walk

Suggested connections by bus

Originally launched in the early 1990s as the High Weald Walk with a guide produced by Kent County Council, the Tunbridge Wells Circular Walk forms a 27.5 mile ring around the town like the rim of a wheel with the town at the centre. In addition there are four link routes that resemble the spokes of the wheel linking the town centre with the rim, in one case involving a short train ride to High Brooms station.

It is therefore possible to walk the entire route based on the town centre by walking out along one spoke, along a section of the rim and back along the next spoke – four walks in total.

However, some of the four walks would be quite long and this approach involves walking every spoke twice, once in each direction. Accordingly, in addition to describing the link routes to facilitate this approach, we have divided the route into four sections easily accessible by public transport, in each case involving a ride out from the town at the start of the walk and another back at the end of the walk. This allows the walk to be done without the use of a car but an alternative is to park at the end of each section and do both bus journeys before starting to walk. Tunbridge Wells is an excellent hub for public transport, both buses and trains. The choice is yours.

## Tunbridge Wells Heritage Walking Trail

Although of no great antiquity – the first building dates from the 17th century – Tunbridge Wells has a colourful history, has been associated with many interesting or famous people and has some very fine architecture. The town is compact and very well suited to exploration on foot – a suitable route is therefore described.

## Walks Through Time

Tunbridge Wells town and the Circular Walk are located at the western end of Tunbridge Wells District. Close to the eastern end of the District lies the ancient market town of Cranbrook, its original prosperity derived from the Wealden cloth trade. In 2012 the Kent High Weald Partnership with Cranbrook in Bloom devised six "Walks Through Time" based on Cranbrook and published a set

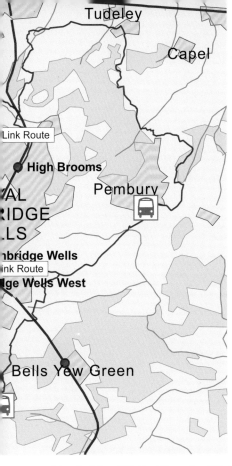

of leaflets describing their routes and the points of interest along them. These leaflets are not now readily available so we have included all the walks in this book with new maps, directions and notes. They have a slightly more remote feel than the Circular Walk and pass through typical Wealden landscape. The paths are also a little less well maintained and waymarked – we are working with Kent County Council to resolve outstanding issues, if necessary using profits from this and our other books. Meanwhile we have included additional detail in the route descriptions and maps to help you find your way.

## Maps

The maps that follow have been carefully prepared to meet your needs and at the time of publication are likely to be more up to date than available Ordnance Survey maps. That will change of course and in any case you may want maps that cover a wider area. For walking, Explorer maps (1:25,000) are far superior to Landranger maps (1:50,000). The Explorer maps that cover the routes are:

**Tunbridge Wells Circular Walk:** 147 (Sevenoaks & Tonbridge), 136 (High Weald) and 135 (Ashdown Forest)

**Walks Through Time:** 136 (High Weald), 137 (Ashford) and 125 (Romney Marsh, Rye & Winchelsea

## Planning and Equipment

From spring to autumn, these are not difficult walks. The Heritage Trail is straightforward at any time of year. However, in a wet winter you are pretty certain to encounter some mud on the other walks, especially those from Cranbrook. Mud and clay have played a major role in shaping the delightful landscape that is the Weald by forcing farming to be relatively small-scale and making travel challenging until quite recent times so that small but charming settlements survived relatively unspoiled. Local clay has also been used to make the red brick and tiles that make many Wealden buildings so special. We should be thankful for the mud and accept that following wet weather we should wear a stout pair of boots that will require a good wash after the walk.

Apart from boots, which are preferable to shoes at any time of year, you will only need the usual kit of sun cream, sun hat, waterproofs, rucksack, mobile phone, water and perhaps lunch – although there is usually a pub or other eating facility to be found at some point.

Of course we hope that you will also carry this guide, but if not then take the Ordnance Survey Explorer maps mentioned above, which are useful anyway in case you decide to venture off the described route.

## Safety

Walking, especially in lowland areas, is a pretty safe activity. The biggest danger is when crossing or briefly walking along a busy road with no pavement or verge, which is sometimes unavoidable. Keep to the right-hand side and be prepared to walk in single file. At a sharp right-hand bend it may be safer to cross to the left-hand side of the road and cross back after the bend. For more safety advice see www.ramblers.org.uk/advice/safety.

Wherever you walk, you should consider taking precautions against ticks that may transmit Lyme disease.

## The 2020 Covid-19 Outbreak

Details of facilities such as pubs, cafés and tourist attractions were researched before the Covid-19 outbreak. At the time of publication there remains uncertainty about how many of these will reopen and when. It is also uncertain how public transport, particularly buses, will be affected in the long term. Public transport arrangements should therefore be checked at www.travelinesoutheast.org.uk before you set out. Please also check the Kent Ramblers web site for any changes that we become aware of.

## Kent High Weald Partnership

The Kent High Weald Partnership is a non-profit organisation whose aim is to link people with nature in their local green spaces. This is achieved through working with communities mainly in the borough of Tunbridge Wells to deliver events and volunteer task days. They also focus on outdoor education, habitat management and run projects that use the power of nature to help people feel better, both physically and mentally. For more information visit khwp.org.uk.

## The High Weald Area of Outstanding Natural Beauty

The unique and precious landscape of the High Weald has since 1983 been recognised by its status as one of England's 34 AONBs. A partnership of the local authorities and other organisations – the High Weald AONB Joint Advisory Committee – was set up in 1989 to help manage this national asset and is supported by a small team based in Flimwell, which advises on how to conserve and enhance the area's distinctive landscape character. More information about the High Weald AONB can be found at highweald.org.

## Explore Kent

Explore Kent is a Kent County Council led partnership with public, private and voluntary sector partners that promotes the wonderful natural environment that Kent has to offer. Its web site (explorekent.org) features 150 walking and cycling routes, over 200 parks and green spaces.

# Evolution of the Landscape

## Geology

### The Geology of the Weald

The Weald is very much defined in terms of underlying geology. Most of the solid rocks exposed in Kent and large parts of Sussex were laid down under water during a geological period known as the Cretaceous which began around 144 million years ago.

Beneath the rocks of the Cretaceous are older rocks of the Jurassic and earlier geological periods including coal measures that were once exploited in the collieries of east Kent.

As the Cretaceous began, the platform of Jurassic and older rocks in the area had subsided and been covered by the waters of a large estuary whose boundaries changed over the millennia so that sediments washed down by the river sometimes settled in freshwater and sometimes in saltwater.

Over time huge beds of sandstones, mudstones and occasionally limestones built up until, around 97 million years ago, much of the area was inundated by the sea and thick layers of chalk built up from the bodies of marine creatures that settled to the seabed.

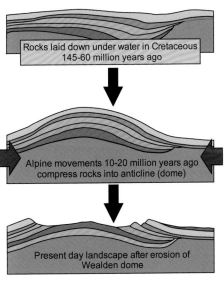

Figure 1

Figure 1 (top) shows the sequence of the beds that had built up by the end of the Cretaceous around 66 million years ago.

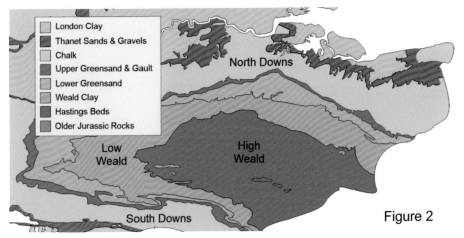

Figure 2

At this time the uplift of the Weald began, being initially very limited but sufficient to raise the area above sea level and so halt the deposition of the chalk.

Gradually the pressure from the tectonic processes creating the Alps increased until by 15 to 20 million years ago a roughly west to east anticline (ridge) was forming. At the same time there was pressure from the west due to the opening of the North Atlantic so that the net result was an elongated dome that covered not just south east England but also what is now the English Channel and parts of north west Europe – Figure 1 (middle).

As this dome was eroded away the oldest rocks were exposed in the centre and the youngest rocks at the edge forming a series of concentric oval rings – Figures 1 (bottom) and 2. The chalk was the outermost ring, forming the North and South Downs and corresponding outcrops on the other side of the Channel. The inner rings – the Weald Clay and the Hastings Beds – are often referred to respectively as the Low Weald and the High Weald.

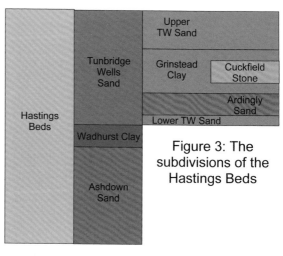

Figure 3: The subdivisions of the Hastings Beds

## The Geology of the Tunbridge Wells Area

The Tunbridge Wells Circular Walk falls wholly within the High Weald and the rocks are those of the Hastings Beds. Within the Hastings Beds we find alternating beds of clays (consolidated to mudstones) and sandstones – Figure 3. The character of these layers, the differential exposure resulting from faulting during and after the Alpine uplift and the pattern of weathering combine to create the intimate and appealing Wealden landscape.

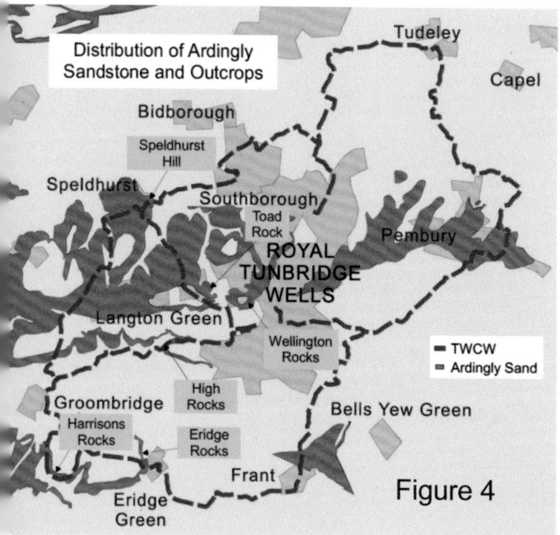

Perhaps the most conspicuous of the Wealden rocks is the hard Ardingly sandstone which is exposed in many places close to the route of the Tunbridge Wells Circular Walk. The pattern of outcrops is shown in Figure 4.

Figure 4

These are often weathered into interesting shapes such as the famous Toad Rock at Rustall and the High Rocks between Tunbridge Wells and Groombridge. The sandstone is popular with climbers but is easily damaged so that access has to be strictly managed.

Eridge Rocks end abruptly at their northern edge while High Rocks end abruptly at their southern edge. In the area between, which includes the large expanse of Broadwater Forest and the village of Groombridge, only the older Ashdown sandstone is exposed. The Ashdown beds have been raised here to the level of the surrounding Ardingly beds by a pair of major faults, the North Groombridge fault and the South Groombridge fault. Figure 5 shows these and other faults that are key influences on the landscape of the area.

Both the sandstones and mudstones contain iron ores and so the area has been home to a thriving iron industry (described more fully in our guide to *Three River Valley Walks in West Kent*). Although the industry is long gone, it has left its mark on the landscape, not least in the ponds created to store the water that powered the furnaces and forges.

Oak trees grow well in Wealden clay which also makes beautiful red bricks and tiles. The timber framed houses made from the oaks, then roofed and clad in tiles and often infilled with the bricks, are characteristic of the Weald and contribute significantly to its visual appeal.

Figure 5: The Development of Faulting in the Tunbridge Wells Area

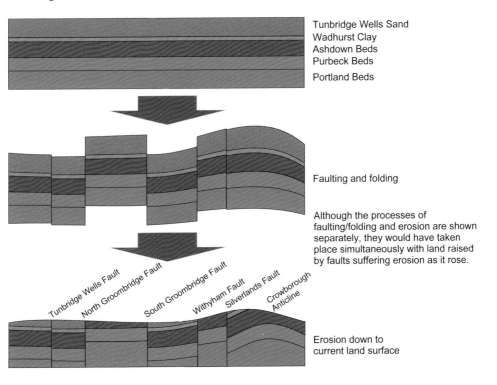

# Section 1: Frant to Groombridge (7 miles)

There is no natural place to start a circular walk. We have chosen Frant because it offers opportunities for on-street parking and a frequent bus service to and from Tunbridge Wells. There are also two pubs – the George Inn and the Abergavenny Arms. There is even a Post Office and shop with café.

This section of the walk coincides with the High Weald Landscape Trail and as far as Eridge Green it coincides with a waymarked "Wealden Walk". You can therefore follow the waymarks for these walks as well as those for the Tunbridge Wells Circular Walk.

Starting from village green, cross to west side of road and head down footway alongside A267 noting entrance drive to Shernfold Park on left as you pass. Take footpath on the

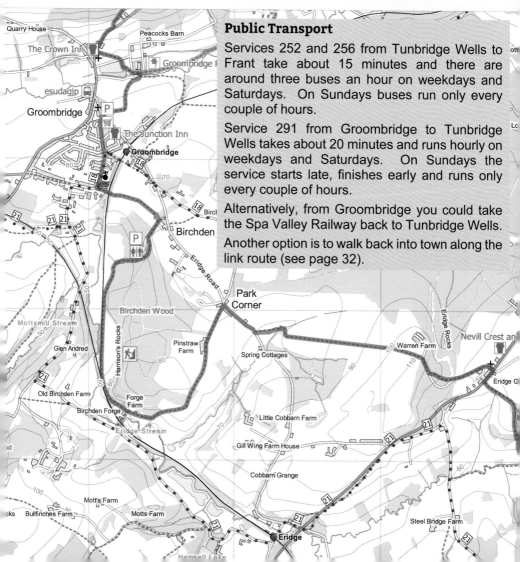

## Public Transport

Services 252 and 256 from Tunbridge Wells to Frant take about 15 minutes and there are around three buses an hour on weekdays and Saturdays. On Sundays buses run only every couple of hours.

Service 291 from Groombridge to Tunbridge Wells takes about 20 minutes and runs hourly on weekdays and Saturdays. On Sundays the service starts late, finishes early and runs only every couple of hours.

Alternatively, from Groombridge you could take the Spa Valley Railway back to Tunbridge Wells.

Another option is to walk back into town along the link route (see page 32).

right downhill between fences alongside telephone exchange (set back from the road with a parking area in front). At bottom bear left through gate into deer park and head downhill, following waymarks. Enter woodland through a gate and follow rough, sometimes muddy, track until you reach a lake. Turn left across bridge over stream at end of lake, go through pedestrian gate on right just before field gate and alongside fence to corner. Bear left and follow track until you meet stony track at bridge. Turn right uphill across parkland offering fine views of large lake on right – and perhaps, if the surrounding trees have not grown too large, the top of Saxonbury Tower on the skyline to the left. At far side of parkland follow stony track forward, crossing another track, then after just a few metres take footpath on right. Follow this through woodland to emerge at stile. Don't go over the stile but bear right across stream then quite steeply uphill parallel to hedge on right. Continue to the A26 at Eridge Green.

Cross road and turn right. After 100 metres, immediately before church, turn left along asphalt track. (If you wish to detour to the Nevill Crest and

Gun for refreshment, continue along the A26 past the church and you will soon reach it on your left.)

Follow the track to a small car park at Eridge Rocks. A couple of metres beyond the car park, take path on right through bracken until it rejoins asphalt track. Turn right and, immediately after woodland on left ends, take path on left passing well to left of Warren Farm and soon heading downhill across the middle of a very large field.

At far edge of field turn right along field edge to corner, descend to cross footbridge and follow right hand edge of field to lane. Turn right and at top of hill at Park Corner take track on left. Pass Pinstraw Farm and carry on between buildings at Forge Farm then on through trees to emerge into open meadow with Harrison's Rocks on right and Spa Valley Railway on left. Follow path below railway then turn right towards car park and toilet block for climbers in Birchden Wood. Follow track uphill along right hand side of car park, bearing left at corner and climbing to meet asphalt drive.

Turn right and at end of first field on left take path on left between fence and hedge. Follow path to bridge across railway and up to Corseley

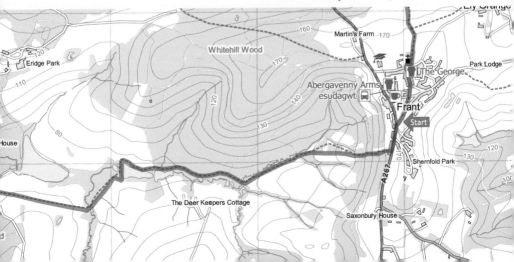

Road by school. Turn right past church, downhill to Station Road then left to mini-roundabout and bus stop – or bear right across Station Road and through car park to embark on the next section of the walk.

# Places of Interest

## Shernfold Park

The current Grade II listed house was built in 1855 by P Ashburnham. During World War II it was used by the Waifs and Strays Society for the evacuation of girls from their St Mary's Home in Cheam. It appears now to have been divided up into apartments.

The previous house on the site was owned from 1820 to 1836 by Lieutenant-Colonel John By, an engineer who built a military canal from the Ottawa River to Lake Ontario in Canada. The town he built to house the workers was at first called Bytown but the name was later changed to Ottawa. By had earlier been in charge of various gunpowder works including that at Faversham. It is probably coincidence that the house had been built in 1790 by Charles Pigou, a gunpowder manufacturer.

Eridge park

## Eridge Park

The current Georgian-style house was built in the late 1930s to replace the flamboyant neo-Gothic Eridge Castle that had been inspired by Horace Walpole's Strawberry Hill House. The Castle had been begun in 1787 by Henry Nevill, 2nd Earl of Abergavenny, who also built a crenellated wall to hide from the Castle's view an estate farm – ever since known as Sham Farm. A subsequent Nevill built Saxonbury Tower, a folly a couple of miles to the south close to the site of an iron age fort.

The park itself is said to be the the oldest enclosed deer park in the country. The lakes were created in the 16th century to hold water to power iron works on the estate.

## Eridge Green

The village, minus green, was moved here in the late 18th century as its original location spoiled the view from the then new Castle. Every house bears the Abergavenny motif, leaving the villagers in no doubt who owned their homes.

Old Eridge Castle

## Eridge Rocks

An outcrop of Ardingly sandstone where there is an uneas balance between the interests of climbers and the desire to preserve fragile rock surfaces and the unusual plants that live in and between them. The Rocks are a Site of Special Scientific Interest and a nature reserve belonging to the Sussex Wildlife Trust.

Abergavenny Motif

## Park Corner

The house on the corner as you turn left at Park Corner bears the coat of arms of the Goldsmiths' Company who used to own the land in this area including nearby Pinstraw Farm. The house was once a pub, The Goldsmiths' Arms.

## Birchden Forge and Harrison's Rocks

Harrison's Rocks are named after William Harrison, a leading figure in the Wealden iron industry until his death in 1745. Harrison owned interests in many furnaces and forges across the Weald, including Birchden Forge which you pass just before reaching the Rocks and Hamsell Furnace a kilometre to the south east. Furnaces and forges often operated in pairs with the furnace smelting the iron out of the ore and the forge processing the iron further to reduce carbon content and remove slag. Both operations required water power – for the bellows in the furnace and for the hammer in the forge. The large amounts of water needed would be stored in furnace or hammer ponds, many of which are still significant

Harrison's Rocks

features of the Wealden landscape – the pond for both furnace and forge here is marked on the map as Hamsell Lake.

When coke became widely used for smelting iron the Wealden industry, which used much more expensive charcoal, disappeared and Harrison's Rocks were opened as a very popular tourist attraction. They later developed into an important centre for rock climbing and many who later went on to tackle major mountains such as Everest learnt their ropes here, including Chris Bonington.

## Glen Andred

The house was built in the 1860s for artist, geologist and landscape designer Edward William Cooke with a character reflecting the Arts and Crafts movement. However, it is the garden designed by Cooke that has listed Grade II status, although not all of the original garden survives. The house and garden have been divided up and are in multiple ownership.

## Groombridge Place

The moated manor house dates from 1662. It featured as Longbourne in the 2005 film adaptation of Pride and Prejudice. Christopher Wren helped design the house and diarist John Evelyn helped design the garden. The house is not currently open to the public but the gardens are a tourist attraction focusing on events likely to interest families with younger children.

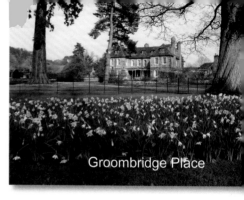

Groombridge Place

# A Brief History of the Weald

The Weald is defined primarily by geology (see page 7) and secondarily by the landscapes that result from that geology. At the centre of the Wealden dome we have the Hastings beds – alternating sandstones and clays that form the High Weald. Surrounding the Hastings beds in a huge oval (truncated by the English Channel but continuing on the other side) is the Wealden clay that forms the Low Weald.

Like most of Britain, the area became wooded after the last glaciation ended. By the time of the Roman invasion, ancient Britons had cleared substantial tracts of woodland for agriculture across most of the country. However, although there had been some woodland clearance in the Weald, its heavy soils were generally better suited to woodland and grazing than to crops and the area remained the most wooded in Britain.

During the Roman occupation the Weald became the centre of a large-scale iron industry – perhaps the second largest such centre in the Empire – and the potential for production of iron is thought to have been one of the reasons for the Roman invasion. The available ore, iron carbonate from the Wadhurst clay, was relatively easy to smelt with an average iron content of 40%; the forest produced excellent charcoal and the clay could be used for furnace construction. By the end of the Roman occupation iron production in the Weald had already declined substantially, perhaps due to exhaustion of easily accessible ore and over exploitation of the woodland, and thereafter it virtually ceased.

Occupation of the Weald was very limited for several centuries and the wood reclaimed much of the land cleared by the Romans. When the Saxons and Jutes arrived the area was characterised as the Andredesweald, the term "weald" or "wald" signifying not just trees but more varied wild country with uncultivated clearings too.

For many more centuries the Weald was exploited on a seasonal basis. Farmers from outside the area, both to the north and the south, would drive animals into the woods in summer and autumn for pasture. In particular pigs would be brought in to feed on beech mast and acorns – the swine pastures were known as dens and "den" as a place-name ending is very common in the

Kentish Weald – the corresponding term in Sussex is "fold". The droveways created by the herdsmen, gradually worn deeper into the landscape by feet and trotters, are a lasting legacy with many still traceable as either modern roads or delightful footpaths.

Weavers' Cottages, Goudhurst

Gradually attempts were made to clear the woodland and establish farms. The Wealden soils suited a pattern of small fields on small farms employing a mixed farming system that integrated woodlands, grasslands, orchards and arable. The farms produced field crops, fruit, pigs, timber and meat and milk from cattle and sheep grazing on wildflower-rich grasslands. The farming methods that evolved in medieval times changed little until the 18th century and even then Wealden farmers were slow to abandon their tried and tested ways. In consequence the Weald has avoided the worst excesses of the intensive farming practices that have taken hold elsewhere since the end of World War II. The Weald now boasts one of the best preserved medieval landscapes in Europe and if the land is managed well it will continue to yield quality food that is sustainably produced.

From the 13th to the 17th centuries there was a thriving woollen industry and in Tudor and Stuart times there was a huge revival of the iron industry with the introduction of the blast furnace. The wealth generated by these industries paid for some of the finest buildings in the area – the cloth houses and ironmasters' houses. Many of these were timber-framed and hugely enhance the Wealden landscape to this day.

Sunken Track

For nearly 2000 years the Weald had been regarded as a challenging landscape and little valued by outsiders but in the 18th century it came to be appreciated as home to a way of life that elsewhere had been or soon would be extinguished by the industrial and agricultural revolutions. Here was the last surviving vestige of old England and here the wealthy began to buy properties and build houses to enjoy the landscape and scenery – which reminded some of the Italian landscapes they had seen on the Grand Tour. By and large the roads remained terrible and development was confined to parts of the Weald close to the few good turnpikes. Difficulty of access remained an issue well into the 20th century, helping to preserve a landscape that can only be fully appreciated on foot. The Weald is a walker's paradise – at least once spring arrives and the mud dries out.

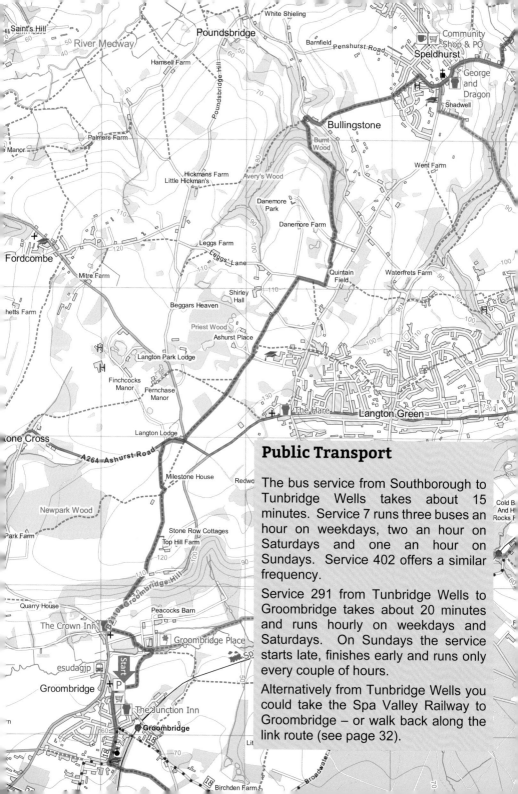

## Public Transport

The bus service from Southborough to Tunbridge Wells takes about 15 minutes. Service 7 runs three buses an hour on weekdays, two an hour on Saturdays and one an hour on Sundays. Service 402 offers a similar frequency.

Service 291 from Tunbridge Wells to Groombridge takes about 20 minutes and runs hourly on weekdays and Saturdays. On Sundays the service starts late, finishes early and runs only every couple of hours.

Alternatively from Tunbridge Wells you could take the Spa Valley Railway to Groombridge – or walk back along the link route (see page 32).

## Section 2: Groombridge to Southborough (9.7 miles)

Leave the village car park at farthest edge of the

**Correction**

Page 17: Length of Section 2 is 6.1 miles = 9.7 km

and bear
en fences
ce. Cross
footbridge over river Grom and turn left between river and moat. Bear right alongside iron railings towards steps (in line with bridge over moat) leading up to pond; at top turn right along pond edge and cross asphalt track. Bear left uphill across field passing to right of church to Groombridge Hill opposite Crown Inn.

Cross road and turn right uphill then take path on left immediately after 50 mph speed restriction signs. Climb up through woodland, offering fine displays of bluebells in spring. At top bear right and left onto path between fences, later widening between hedges. Continue past one or two field gates to wide track at T-junction. Bear right and after 30 metres bear left through the leftmost of two field gates to resume original northerly direction along track between hedges to road (A264).

Turn right through roadside nature reserve to road junction at Langton Lodge. Cross both roads and take path through gate across field towards right hand edge of wood. Pass to right of wood and along field edge to corner and use two stiles to cross another path. Maintain direction, crossing first drive to Ashurst Place and then drive to Shirley Hall. Cross two fields to Leggs' Lane.

Turn right and after a couple of hundred metres take path on left down step and through gate. Follow left hand edge of field for 150 metres then go through gap on left and follow path between fences to drive for Danemore Park. Cross and follow path downhill into wood (where the bluebells in spring are spectacular). Follow path through wood, eventually descending to a footbridge across the stream. On the other side climb steeply to a junction at the highest point and bear right between houses to Bullingstone Lane.

Turn right and after 100 metres take an uphill track on the left. Follow track, ignoring all turns, until you reach Penshurst Road at Speldhurst.

Cross road, turn right then follow road round to left past church (the George & Dragon is on the opposite side of the road should you seek refreshment). Here link route from Tunbridge Wells joins main route.

Go downhill past church to road junction and cross very carefully to footway on right hand side of Speldhurst Hill then head downhill. Take not first but second path on left along track leading down to the old water mill. Past the mill, take path uphill to lane.

Turn right for 50 metres then take path up steps on left. Follow path between fences, ignoring left and right turns, without change of direction until path emerges into open field and bears right to gap in hedge and gate to lane.

Cross lane and continue in same direction until path emerges in a housing estate. Go forward and at first junction turn left and immediately right. At T-junction turn left then take first right. At first bend take path on left downhill past play area to Holden Corner. Turn left in front of pond and right at end of pond and at corner take

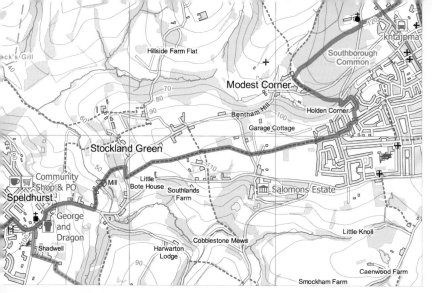

track on left uphill through woods to Victoria Road at Modest Corner.

Cross road and go along lane with houses on left and woodland on right.

At corner, turn right uphill along path into woodland and keep climbing in same direction to emerge beside the church at Southborough.

# Points of Interest

## Groombridge Green

Groombridge straddles the Kent/Sussex border and the green is in the Kent or northerly part of the village. The green is characterised by lime trees, the row of tile-hung cottages that includes the Crown Inn and the unusual brick church across the road. A drive through a stone gateway leads to Burrswood.

## Burrswood

The estate was bought in 1831 by David Salomons who also owned Broom Hill Cottage, now the Salomons Estate (see later), and had a house built by

The Crown, Groombridge Green

the architect Decimus Burton. It was described in 1838 as "a handsome structure, chiefly in the Elizabethan style…" but others might consider some more recent additions including the church rather lacking in aesthetic appeal. From 1948 until 2019 it was used as a Christian healing and conference centre, there was a popular tea room and the public were free to walk in the fine grounds. The trust running the centre ran into financial difficulties in 2019, closed all facilities and put the estate up for sale. The new owners seem likely to convert

Burnt Wood

the buildings into residential accommodation and the future of public access is uncertain.

## Langton Lodge

The lodge stands beside what was once the main drive to Ashurst Park, a large early 19th century house later renamed Ashurst Manor (as it is still shown on OS maps) and more recently still Fernchase Manor. The lodge bears the monogram GF which refers to George Hanbury Field (1835-1901) and appears on many houses belonging to the original estate which he owned. The estate has been divided up and within the park a nursing home (Ashurst Park) and a private hospital has been built.

## Ashurst Place

This red brick building was until very recently a care home. At the time of writing the builders are in, perhaps converting it to luxury apartments.

## Shirley Hall

This fine stuccoed early 19th century building with brick chimneys was built on the site of Sherlocks Farm, reputed to be mentioned in the Domesday Book although my searches have failed to find it. The house was used as a grain store between the wars, by the army in World War II and subsequently restored and converted into apartments.

## Quintain Field

The field is thought to have been used for medieval jousting practice. A quintain was a horizontal wooden bar rotating on a vertical wooden pole; on one end of the bar was a wooden target and on the other a bag of sand which would strike the jouster if he was too slow.

## Danemore Park

The Grade II listed 1830s house is approached by an avenue of chestnut with some oak and lime, crossed by this route.

## Burnt Wood and Avery's Wood

Here you walk through a typical Wealden ghyll with steeply wooded sides. You may spot orchids, wood valerian and golden saxifrage but most spectacular are the displays of bluebells each spring.

Bullingstone

## Bullingstone

There are many listed 15th and 16th century houses spaced along Bullingstone Lane.

# Speldhurst

The parish of Speldhurst is one of the oldest hereabouts and was once much larger, encompassing much land that is now in surrounding parishes. The present church was built on the site of several predecessors. The medieval church was struck by lightning and destroyed in 1791. Its replacement was of poor quality and had to be demolished in 1870. The present church was built by John Oldrid Scott, son of George Gilbert Scott who championed the Gothic revival, and there is a notable series of windows by the Pre-Raphaelite artist Edward Burne-Jones.

Speldhurst Church

While opinions vary on the merits of the church building, its location is indisputably splendid at the edge of a sandstone plateau and from its door one sees nothing but fine ancient buildings including, across the road, a picturesque old inn, the George and Dragon.

The village has a thriving community shop and post office, set up in 2019 when it was threatened with closure on the retirement of the owner.

## George & Dragon

A public house for over 200 years, this Grade II* listed building from the late 15th century has many exposed beams that betray its origin as a late medieval hall house. At the time of writing the pub is closed and the lease up for sale.

## Speldhurst Mill

Also known as Taylor's Mill, this is one of Kent's best preserved water powered corn mills. The wheel, which was originally driven by water pouring into buckets attached to it, can still be seen although it has deteriorated significantly in the last decade and it is not certain what its fate will be following a redevelopment of the site as residential accommodation that is taking place at the time of writing. The mill pond is still intact and full of water.

The Salomons Water Tower

## Salomons Estate

Broom Hill cottage was bought by David Salomons in 1829. When he sold Burrswood (see earlier) in 1851 he rebuilt Broomhill and Decimus Burton may again have been the architect. His nephew, Sir David Lionel Salomons, built the nearby water tower (see photograph) to house an astronomical telescope and organised the first motor show – the Horseless Carriage Exhibition of 1895.

For a while the building belonged to Canterbury Christ Church College and was used as a conference and training centre. More recently the mansion has been converted into a hotel and wedding venue with the outbuildings let to various businesses but there is still public access to the grounds and a small museum. Visitor parking may be easier at weekends.

Holden Pond

## Holden Pond

Possibly a mill pond. Once heavily polluted by effluent from a tannery to the east which dated back at least to 1720, probably produced leather for the local trade of cricket ball manufacture and closed in 1922. Now in good health and popular for fishing (permit required).

## Modest Corner

The name may derive from 14th century resident John Mode. A spring here was the source for one of Kent's earliest water supply undertakings established in 1885 by Southborough Urban District Council.

## Southborough Common

The common has a long and colourful history. From the 5th to the 9th centuries the area was swine pasture belonging to the Manor of Wrotham. In 1522-23 Henry VIII granted the Manor of Southborough to Sir Thomas More, but took it back in 1530-31 when More was executed for failing to support Henry as head of the Church of England. Henry then granted the Manor to George, brother of Anne Boleyn, only to take it back once more when George was executed for "too close an association with Anne".

Over the centuries the common was used for grazing by local landowners. In the 19th century it was used for a number of industrial purposes. There were a "post" windmill and a smithy on the common and two laundries at Modest Corner – the washed clothes were spread out on the common to dry. Charcoal was produced, possibly for the gunpowder works at Old Forge Farm.

The playing of cricket on the common dates back at least to 1794 and the manufacture of cricket balls was one of Southborough's main industries in the 19th and early 20th centuries.

From the 19th century grazing on the common reduced and leisure use increased. With the cessation of grazing the common became more wooded and scrub took over much of the ground. A management plan is now in place that will see the removal of scrub, especially holly, so that the woodland will become much more open and although looking bare initially will develop a much richer ecology.

Southborough Church

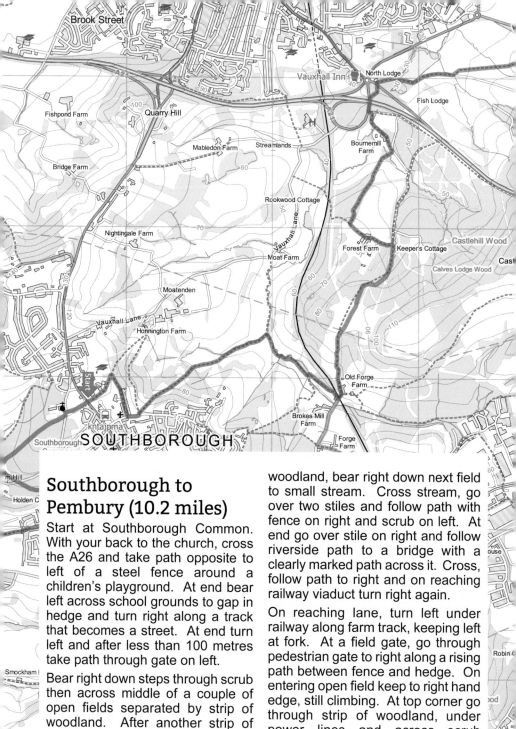

# Southborough to Pembury (10.2 miles)

Start at Southborough Common. With your back to the church, cross the A26 and take path opposite to left of a steel fence around a children's playground. At end bear left across school grounds to gap in hedge and turn right along a track that becomes a street. At end turn left and after less than 100 metres take path through gate on left.

Bear right down steps through scrub then across middle of a couple of open fields separated by strip of woodland. After another strip of woodland, bear right down next field to small stream. Cross stream, go over two stiles and follow path with fence on right and scrub on left. At end go over stile on right and follow riverside path to a bridge with a clearly marked path across it. Cross, follow path to right and on reaching railway viaduct turn right again.

On reaching lane, turn left under railway along farm track, keeping left at fork. At a field gate, go through pedestrian gate to right along a rising path between fence and hedge. On entering open field keep to right hand edge, still climbing. At top corner go through strip of woodland, under power lines and across scrub

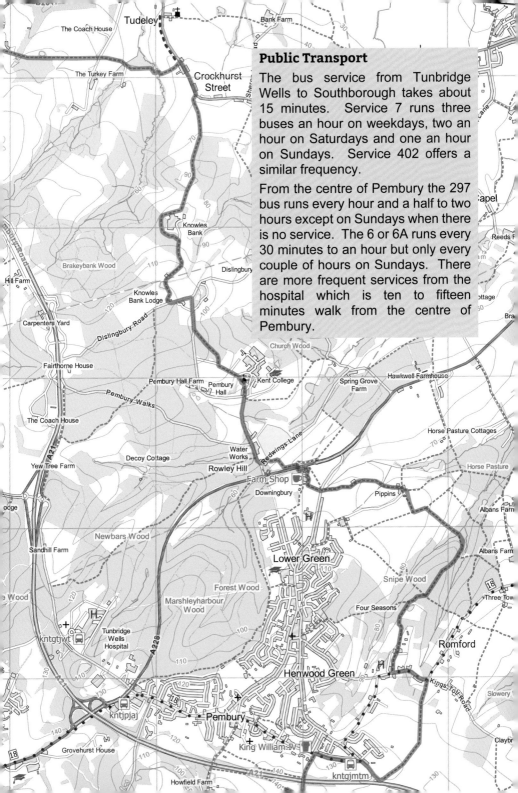

## Public Transport

The bus service from Tunbridge Wells to Southborough takes about 15 minutes. Service 7 runs three buses an hour on weekdays, two an hour on Saturdays and one an hour on Sundays. Service 402 offers a similar frequency.

From the centre of Pembury the 297 bus runs every hour and a half to two hours except on Sundays when there is no service. The 6 or 6A runs every 30 minutes to an hour but only every couple of hours on Sundays. There are more frequent services from the hospital which is ten to fifteen minutes walk from the centre of Pembury.

towards more woodland. Follow path which bears right then left down to a lane.

Turn left uphill and pass to right of converted oast at Forest Farm. At end of open field on right, turn right along track just inside wood. Follow this track, gradually descending (and with a splendid display of bluebells in the wood to the left in spring) to asphalt track. Turn left and follow valley bottom to slip road. Don't cross at the pedestrian crossing but continue along same side of slip road under the A21 to take path through trees on right. On reaching the A26, cross carefully and go through gate leading into Somerhill Park.

Follow driveway past lake and when signs indicate bear left uphill away from the driveway. Follow path to dropping-off point for Somerhill School. At far side, bear left for a few metres then right through a path between high stone walls that prevent views of the house and grounds. At end of walls, continue through wood then across middle of field downhill to junction of farm tracks. Take track opposite downhill and soon after it bears right, turn left along left hand edge of field. At corner, turn right and soon take path into wood on left. Cross footbridge over stream then bear right and left to climb across middle of field to road, B2017.

Cross carefully and turn right past houses and Indian restaurant. When road turns left, cross road (very carefully!) to track in corner and climb first through trees then alongside woods on left and open fields with fine views on the right. On reaching gate to Knowles Bank, turn right along path that completes a half circle through woodland round house. At far side

turn right up asphalt drive and follow to lane.

Turn left and at junction turn right downhill. As road starts to climb again, take path into woodland on left (fine bluebells in spring). Emerging in grounds of Kent College, turn left along asphalt track but soon bear right off track into churchyard. On far side of churchyard, leave through main entrance down lane and past waterworks at bottom. As road starts to climb again, turn left along Redwings Lane and after pair of houses on right take path up bank on right. Bear left uphill to stile then turn right uphill between fences. At top turn left along top of field then up bank onto track. Turn right across bridge over A228 then immediately left between hedge and large pylon.

Turn right, passing door of farm shop and café where you could stop for refreshment if open, then follow asphalt drive, soon bearing left to Maidstone Road. Cross to farm track opposite; follow through orchards towards substantial group of buildings including a triple-cowled oast house (Pippins). Keep to the left of the oasts then bear right across concrete track to unmade track. After a few metres take path up bank on right. Follow right hand edge of orchard.

At top go through gap in hedge and turn left then take first turn on right downhill with abandoned apple orchard on left and line of alders on right. At bottom cross bridge over stream (which, it is claimed, used to drive Keyes Mill a short distance downstream) and follow track uphill, soon bearing right. Shortly meet High Weald Landscape Trail joining from the left and for the rest of the walk you will be following both routes. Continue forward through woods (much of it chestnut coppice) until as the path starts to descend there is a left turn opposite a green gate marked Snipe Wood Farm on the right. Take the left turn and follow track to lane.

Turn left past several houses and at junction of lanes take footpath on the right uphill through trees then across open field. At top go through hedge and along right hand edge of field. At corner bear right over stile then turn left along path down to A21. Turn right up road and at fork keep left to bus stop where you can get a bus to Tunbridge Wells. To continue along the TWCW, go past the bus stop looking for a path on the left (or continue a little further for the King William IV public house on the right).

# Points of Interest

## Old Forge Farm

From 1552 until 1573 the South Frith ironworks, consisting of a forge near Forge Farm and the Vauxhall Furnace three quarters of a mile down the same stream, were operated by wealthy ironmaster Davy Willard. Willard operated up to six ironworks in the area and took part in the Wyatt rebellion against Queen Mary's marriage to King Philip of Spain in 1554.

Forest Farm

There is no evidence that the Vauxhall Furnace operated after 1573. Perhaps thereafter the iron for the forge came from the Bournemill furnace – see below. The reduction in smelting capacity may have been necessary because some of the available sources of wood for charcoal had been exhausted. All remains of the forge were destroyed when the railway viaduct was built in 1846 but the site of Vauxhall furnace is still indicated on the Explorer map by the words "Pond Bay" for the dam that stored the water that powered the bellows for the furnace. Also marked on the map nearby is Minepit Wood so it was likely here that the shallow pits were dug to extract the iron ore.

## Bournemill Farm

There was a blast furnace here, operated by Davy Willard and then his two sons, from around 1560 until at least 1599. Unusually, no armaments were cast, only sows of iron to be worked in a forge for commercial and domestic use.

## Wildlife Ladders

As you are about to walk under the A21 look up and to the left. Climbing from the embankment and snaking high under the underpass are mesh

Lake at Somerhill

passageways, the vertical ones containing thick ropes. These are presumably to allow wildlife such as dormice to cross the A21 safely although it is not clear how wildlife would know their purpose and I've never seen them being used.

## Somerhill

This Grade I listed Jacobean mansion is notable in the history of architecture as marking the beginning of the transition from the medieval layout with the hall running the length of the building and being the main living room to the modern layout where the hall is somewhere to hang your hat and coat and pass through on the way to other rooms. Somerhill is laid out in an H plan with the hall running through the "bar" from front to back. The house is built of dressed stone which is also unusual for the period (1611-13).

Somerhill

The house is now occupied by three schools and is not open to the public except occasionally for Tunbridge Wells Heritage Open Days.

## Church of All Saints, Tudeley

The church can be visited by a short detour from the TWCW. The walk along the busy road is not pleasant but there is at the present time a permissive path inside the field on the western side of the road, thanks to the landowner – shown as a red dotted line on the map.

The church is primarily known for stained glass by Marc Chagall, commissioned by the then owners of Somerhill Sir Henry and Lady d'Avigdor Goldsmid, in memory of their daughter who drowned in 1963.

Chagall Windows

## Kent College

An independent day and boarding school for girls, Kent College moved to its present location from Folkestone during World War II to avoid the dangers of the channel coast but was still hit by a V-1 flying bomb. The gaudy sports pitch that has recently sprung up beside the footpath rather detracts from the mellow environment created by the nearby St Peter's church within whose ancient graveyard are more than a dozen Grade II listed headstones and memorials.

Keyes Mill

## Pembury Reservoir

The reservoir, operated by South East Water, takes water from local springs. It is treated on site and stored elsewhere for supply to the Tunbridge Wells area. When the reservoir is full, the water simply overflows into the nearby Alders Stream.

## Keyes Mill

The mill had an overshot wooden water wheel, was painted by J M W Turner in 1796 and is said to have been working at least until 1885 although it is shown as "Herrings Mill (Disused)" on the 1872 Ordnance Survey map.

## Bo-Peep Corner

No one knows the origin of the name. Some say it derives from Bon Pepin, being the French word for "good" and a shortening of Pepingeberia, an old name for Pembury. Others think it might hark back to the days when smuggling was rife in the area and this point on the ridge would have been a good lookout point. Yet others think it is an old term connected with a pillory or lock-up. Whichever you choose, it is nothing to do with the nursery rhyme character now depicted on the smart new black metal sign erected in 2006 to replace a wooden one destroyed by a storm in the winter of 2001-02.

## Pembury

The original village of Pembury (or Pippenbury) was sited around the old church of St Peter's next to Kent College. The modern village centre on the ridge along which the A21 ran until the opening of the bypass in 1988 was known first as Copping Crouch Green and then as Pembury Green. Pembury Green was a popular staging post on the road from London to Hastings which generated employment and resulted in a shift of focus away from Old Pembury. Lord Camden, after whom the chief coaching inn was named, paid for a new church on the ridge.

Pippins

# Pembury to Frant
## (5 miles)

Start on the south side of Hastings Road in Pembury about 100 metres east of the King William IV pub. Take path along the right hand edge of a field and across a footbridge over the A21. Go straight ahead alongside a fence to edge of woodland and turn right between rows of trees – this track is part of the Old Coach Road (see Points of Interest). After 100 metres take path on left out into open pasture.

Head straight downhill to footbridge over stream at bottom. Turn right along track and shortly left at junction. Through short section of woodland, head uphill across pasture with

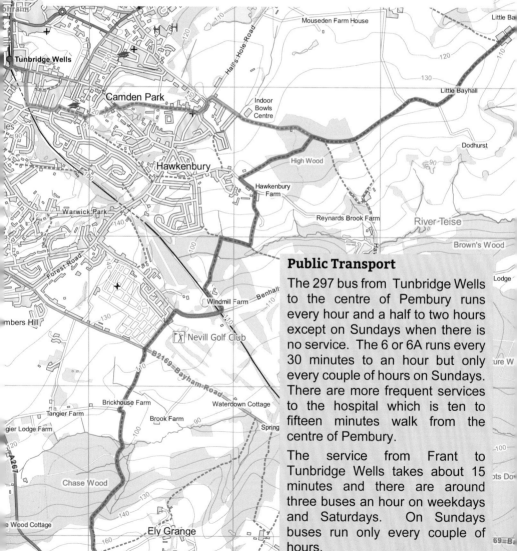

## Public Transport

The 297 bus from Tunbridge Wells to the centre of Pembury runs every hour and a half to two hours except on Sundays when there is no service. The 6 or 6A runs every 30 minutes to an hour but only every couple of hours on Sundays. There are more frequent services to the hospital which is ten to fifteen minutes walk from the centre of Pembury.

The service from Frant to Tunbridge Wells takes about 15 minutes and there are around three buses an hour on weekdays and Saturdays. On Sundays buses run only every couple of hours.

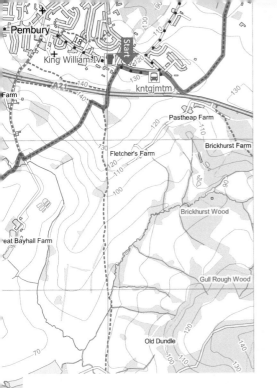

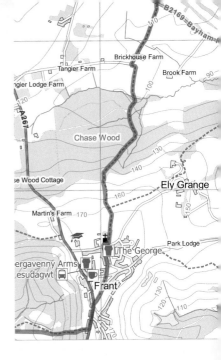

hedge on right then join concrete farm track. Follow track uphill through Little Bayhall Farm and after a mile or so enter High Wood. Follow track as it bears right. When the view ahead shows the track bearing left again, take path on left opposite information panel through coppice then down grassy track past recreation ground on right (seats for lunch) to Hawkenbury Lane.

Turn left for 130 metres then bear right along track at Hawkenbury Farm. At gate across track, bear right down track between hedges then over footbridge across stream to T-junction. Turn right parallel to stream then take left turn downhill to footbridge over stream. Follow path uphill into open area with fenced area on right; at top turn left alongside railway to Benhall Mill Road.

Turn right over railway then immediately past golf course car park on left take path on left past clubhouse (initially through car park) and along right hand edge of course to Bayham Road, B2169.

Bear left across road to farm track and follow through Brickhouse Farm. Turn left and shortly right along path between fences and into woodland. Follow track through wood, crossing a couple of footbridges over Wealden ghylls; at T-junction turn left uphill along broad track. On emerging onto pasture head uphill, through short section of woodland then across more pasture to enter churchyard at Frant. Leave churchyard through unusual lych gate with hexagonal cover then go along road past George Inn to village green.

# Points of Interest

## Old Coach Road

The Old Coach Road ran from Pembury to Bayham Abbey. It enabled the Marquess of Camden, who owned the Bayham Abbey estate and lived in the mansion on the hill above the ruins of the 13th to 15th Premonstratensian Abbey, to avoid the tolls on the Hastings road (now the A21). Some of the Old Coach Road has been turned into a footpath but an application by Kent and Sussex Ramblers in 2008 to establish a right of way for walkers over more of the route was unsuccessful.

## Bayham Abbey

The original abbey was founded around 1207 as a Premonstratensian monastery and dissolved by Cardinal Wolsey in 1525. A new house, also called Bayham Abbey, was built across the river Teise in 1872 by estate owner Lord Camden, by which time the old abbey was a ruin partly modified to the designs of Humphrey Repton to enhance its picturesque qualities. Now owned by English Heritage, the old abbey is open to the public in the summer months.

## Great Bayhall

The original house on the site, a moated medieval manor house built before 1337, belonged to members of the Colepeper family who became prominent in the Wealden iron industry. It was bought by Richard Amherst in the early 17th century and rebuilt by his son, also Richard, as a fashionable country house in the 1650s. The new house fell into disrepair, was demolished in stages and by 1790 had been reduced to a farmhouse which in turn was largely demolished early in the 20th century. The few remains were removed in the 1960s to prevent nuisance from trespassers after a national newspaper published a story about haunting by the ghost of Anne West, a former resident who died in 1803. Afraid of being buried alive, Anne had asked to be buried with a bell and afterwards the bell was heard and locals claimed have seen her corpse walking back to her home.

Old Bayham Abbey in foreground; new Abbey on far horizon

## High Wood

This ancient woodland, much of it chestnut coppice, has a network of paths open to walkers. The bluebells in spring are plentiful.

## Nevill Golf Club

The course was established in 1914 on land in the Abergavenny estate. Having been partly commandeered in the second world war, in 1965 the course was extended and redesigned by Henry Cotton.

St Alban's Lych Gate

## Brickhouse Farm

Bears the Abergavenny motif indicating the building's original ownership as do nearby cottages.

## Frant

The village, whose name indicates a place of ferns or bracken, is situated in the heart of the ancient Wealden forest that even by the time of the Norman conquest had been little settled. Nevertheless, not far away at Saxonbury is an Iron Age hill fort that was probably in use during the century prior to Roman occupation. Apart from the Tudor period when villagers would have been employed in the Wealden iron industry that depended so much on the forest, Frant has always been an agricultural community.

St Alban's church has an unusual hexagonal lych gate incorporating a weather vane which drives a pointer within the gate. Those resting on the seats within the structure can both monitor changes in wind direction and read the commemoration to those who taught in two local schools.

Frant Village Green

## Ely Grange

As you leave the churchyard through the lych gate the lane on the left leads to an imposing gateway. Beyond is the private driveway to Ely Grange where fine houses have stood since at least the 16th century. A new mansion of brick and hung tiles was built in the 1880s but apparently replaced in 1932. For some years after World War II it was Wellcome's Veterinary Research Station and in the 1980s the Vigilant Assurance Company had its offices here. A small residential estate of converted and newly built homes has now developed.

# Link Route from Tunbridge Wells to Groombridge (3.5 miles)

Start from car park at the bottom of Major York's Road, not far from the Pantiles. Take path alongside top of car park. When it divides into two initially parallel paths, take rougher left hand path. On reaching a cross paths with a red brick house on far left corner, turn left down asphalt path to Eridge Road, A26.

Turn right under railway bridge and take first turn right into housing estate. Take the first turn on the right and follow path below railway embankment on right. When path enters wood, keep right at most junctions but don't cross either stream or railway which must both remain on your right.

On reaching lane, turn left past High Rocks and almost immediately after entrance to visitor car park on left, go through small parking area on right onto path under railway and over a bridge across the Grom. Turn left and follow obvious route through woods. At Adam's Well go through metal field gate and uphill then along track to Broom Lane.

Take path immediately opposite alongside the fence around the sewage works. Bear left at Pokehill then right over stile and across field towards Groombridge Place. Pass corner of grounds where there is a children's play area, follow ditch on right for 170 metres then bear left along field edge to house. At footbridge join the main route of the Tunbridge Wells Circular Walk and either turn left over footbridge if going anticlockwise or carry on alongside moat if going clockwise.

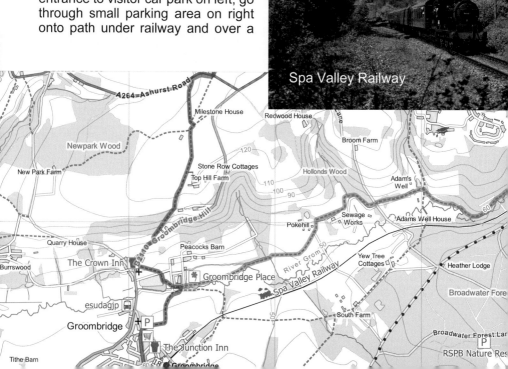

Spa Valley Railway

# Points of Interest on Link Route to Groombridge

## Spa Valley Railway

The railway line between Tunbridge Wells and Eridge was closed in 1985. A preservation society was quickly formed and in 1997 the line was reopened between Groombridge and Tunbridge Wells West stations. It took until 2011 to re-establish the link to Eridge on the main line to Uckfield. There seems little prospect at present of extending the line eastwards from Tunbridge Wells West to the mainline station in the centre of the town but fortunately it is a pleasant walk between the two. Trains don't run every day but they run most days in summer holidays and most weekends.

High Rocks

## High Rocks

This outcrop of Ardingly Sandstone has been turned into a tourist attraction and there is a charge for admission. The rock has been weathered by water seepage and wind erosion into spectacular blocks with wide joints. A series of steps, walkways and rope bridges distinguishes this site from others displaying similar morphological features such as Harrison's Rocks, Eridge Rocks, Happy Valley and Toad Rock, all of which may be visited free of charge on short detours from the route described in this book.

# Link Route from Tunbridge Wells to Speldhurst (2.7 miles)

Start by the Pantiles car park at the bottom of Major York's Road. Take the path alongside the top edge of the car park (the area on your right was a racecourse until the 1850s) and as you approach the western edge of the common bear right to cross the road (Hungersall Park) and head uphill just inside the wooded common with open parkland to the left. Cross the private drive leading to Nevill Park and at the top turn left along the main road, A264.

After passing a right turn (Rusthall Road), cross to the right hand side of the A264 and when the road bears slightly left take the asphalt path straight ahead (you could make a detour to the right to visit the Toad Rock or to the left to visit Happy Valley) leading downhill across Rusthall Common. Cross Rusthall Road and soon reach Lower Green Road. Follow the road downhill then gently left to a junction by The Red Lion. Bear right then cross the road to take an asphalt track uphill keeping right at junctions. Pass *The Junktion* selling a motley collection of tools and equipment, eventually reaching open countryside. Emerging over a stile from the enclosed track, bear right downhill across pasture and into Shadwell Wood.

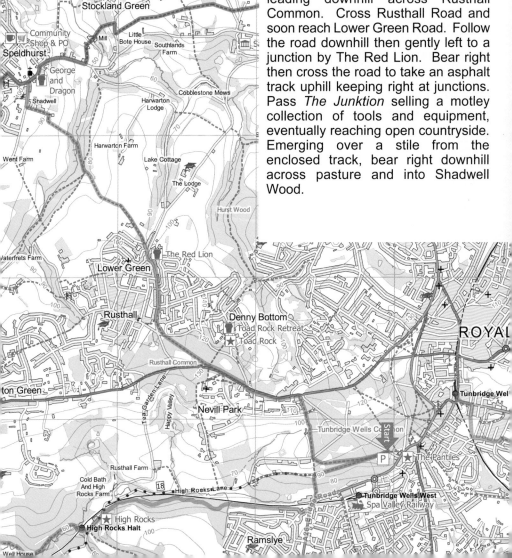

Bear right initially but very shortly fork left downhill to a footbridge then uphill along a clear track leaving the wood and after right and left bends arriving at Langton Road. Turn right passing school on the left and at a junction by the church meet the main route of the TWCW.

# Points of Interest on Link Route to Speldhurst

## Tunbridge Wells and the Pantiles

Tunbridge Wells is the only town in Kent that did not exist in medieval times. It owes its existence to a chalybeate spring discovered in 1606 whose waters were considered to have health enhancing properties. Taking the waters quickly became fashionable but initially there was no accommodation so when Henrietta Maria, Queen of Charles I, visited in 1629 she and her entourage had to camp on the common.

The Pantiles

## Old Racecourse

The racecourse operated from before 1738 until 1851 when it was closed because local residents objected to the drunkenness and riotous behaviour of those attending.

## Rusthall Common and Denny Bottom

The landscape here is much influenced by the underlying geology with many outcrops of Wealden sandstone. Many of the houses at Denny Bottom were built to accommodate workers at the quarry here. Wind erosion during the last ice age has removed softer layers of sandstone leaving harder layers above exposed in unusual formations of which the best known is the Toad Rock.

There is a good selection of shops in Rusthall.

## The Red Lion

According to the original guide to the TWCW, this public house was first licensed around 1415 and is said to be the oldest licensed public house in Kent. However, the Grade II listing by Historic England describes it as a 19th century building. It currently specialises in Thai food. The terrace of cottages opposite with tile hung upper storey is also Grade II listed and described as early 19th century.

## Shadwell

A Grade II listed timber-framed former farmhouse probably from the mid-17th century.

## Link Route High Brooms to Old Forge Farm (1.3 miles)

Leave station on east side, using subway if necessary. Turn left along street to corner and go straight forward between houses onto combined footpath and cycle track. On reaching road go straight across and keep left along footpath between railway on left and industrial estate on right (both fairly well hidden by bushes in summer). On reaching asphalt path turn left across bridge over railway then right into Barnetts Wood nature reserve. Follow asphalt

path downhill and when path ends by a pond go straight forward alongside hedge to gate.

Through gate, cross duckboards over stream and climb along right hand edge of meadow. At this point the chimney from an old brickworks is visible on your left but is so covered in ivy that you may have some difficulty distinguishing it from an unusually uniform tree. On reaching Powder Mill Lane, turn right downhill to railway viaduct and join main route of TWCW. To continue anticlockwise, take path on left immediately before the viaduct. To continue clockwise, go under viaduct.

# Points of Interest on Link Route from High Brooms

## High Brooms

High Brooms, part of Southborough, has long been an industrial area dominated from 1885 until 1968 by the High Brooms Brick and Tile Company. Clay for the tiles and bricks was extracted from a huge pit in which the partial skeleton of an iguanadon was found. Two parts of the pit have accordingly been designated Sites of Special Scientific Interest but the pit has been turned into the High Brooms Industrial Park and the SSSIs are in poor condition.

## Barnett's Wood Local Nature Reserve

Tunbridge Wells Borough's first designated Local Nature Reserve, Barnett's Wood was opened in 1998 comprising a mixture of ancient semi-natural broadleaf woodland and meadows rich in wildflowers.

## Powder Mill Lane

After the closure of the various 16th century forges near Old Forge Farm, the site was redeveloped in 1772 as a gunpowder mill. It had to be rebuilt after an explosion and closed in 1845 after which a corn mill, Broakes Mill, was established and operated until 1923. The large mill pond was immediately to the left of the lane just before the viaduct.

# Link Route Tunbridge Wells to High Wood (1.6 miles)

Start at Tunbridge Wells mainline station. From the entrance in Mount Pleasant Road turn right, cross at the crossing and at the mini roundabout turn left up Grove Hill Road. Cross at the crossing and take the first right along Sutherland Road. At the end bear left diagonally across The Grove (a small park with children's play area) and leave at left hand exit at far corner, going ahead along Claremont Road. At corner cross to Claremont Lodge, turn left then take footpath on the right – this is the first point at which you will see a sign bearing the TWCW waymark.

On reaching street at entrance to Claremont Primary School, take asphalt path on left gently uphill. At lane (Camden Park) turn right then almost immediately left along footpath, later widening to rough drive. On reaching Forest Road, keep left and follow round left hand bend. At second bend cross to Hall's Hole Road then take first right turn along High Woods Lane. At gate continue forward past Indoor Bowls Club and follow asphalt track uphill and into woodland. On reaching post on right bearing waymarks you have reached the main route of the TWCW. To follow the route clockwise, turn right into the woods at the post; to go anticlockwise carry on along the asphalt track.

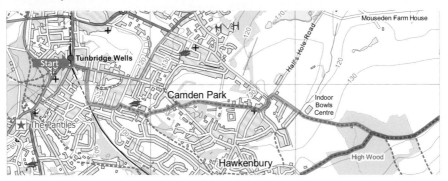

# Point of Interest on Link Route to High Wood

## Claremont Lodge

Note the maroon plaque to Madame Caballero, a high-class courtesan amongst whose clients were both the Duke of Wellington and possibly his elder brother Richard, the Marquess Wellesley. Born Mary Ann Leshley, she was nicknamed "Raffles" from the practice of being raffled to officers and later married Antonio Aureliano Caballero who left her a very wealthy woman, at her death owning much property in Tunbridge Wells.

# Tunbridge Wells Heritage Walking Trail (3.2 miles)

Tunbridge Wells is not an old town – no building predates the 17th century – but from the start it attracted the wealthy and fashionable who have left their mark on the buildings and environment. This trail guides you past a selection of the buildings that are notable either for their architecture or for the people associated with them – and often both.

The walk is 3.2 miles (5.1 km) long but can be considerably shortened by returning along Mount Pleasant Road and the High Street after point 19. The starting point is the Corn Exchange on the lower level of the Pantiles, outside the Tourist Information Centre.

## 1. The Corn Exchange

Originally built in 1801 as a theatre, the building later became the Corn Exchange, at which time the Goddess of the Harvests was installed on the roof, and now houses offices. While the façade is original, the interior has been completely reconstructed. Apart from the Tourist Information Centre which has fairly restricted opening hours, there is no public access.

Edmund Keane

## 2. Edmund Keane

Keane (1787 to 1833) is one of the actors commemorated on a plaque on the Corn Exchange wall. He was an acclaimed Shakespearean actor but his career was badly damaged when he was successfully sued for adultery and a revival was short-lived as his health deteriorated, partly as a consequence of taking stimulants and alcohol. He died at the age of 45.

With the Corn Exchange behind you, turn left along the Lower Walk to the end of the Pantiles, climb to the Upper Walk and turn right.

## 3. The Pantiles

What was then known as "The Walks" was created running south west from the chalybeate spring in 1638 with two rows of wooden buildings which burned down in 1687. The replacement buildings introduced the colonnades and the pantiles, but the latter were largely replaced in 1793. For a while the area was known as the "Royal Parade" but in 1887 the name reverted to the "Pantiles". The original pantiles were made of clay baked in a pan and should not be confused with roofing pantiles whose interlocking S-shaped cross-section allows reduced overlapping and hence lighter roofs. Some sources say a few original pantiles remain they are certainly not easy to find.

## 4. 40-46 The Pantiles

Note the plaque to Richard "Beau" Nash (not to be confused with the Regency architect John Nash who collaborated greatly with Decimus Burton, of whom more later). Beau Nash had established himself as "Master of Ceremonies" at Bath and in 1735 appointed himself additionally to the same role in

Beau Na

The Pantiles

Tunbridge Wells. Here he influenced fashion, enforced a code of behaviour and regulated gambling, an activity to which he was addicted. He had a string of mistresses and continued his functions at both Bath and Tunbridge Wells until his death in 1761.

## 5.    43 The Pantiles

Above the shop on the right, currently a jewellers, is a curved "Musick Gallery" whose iron rails sport the anthemion motif and where musicians serenaded passers-by. A plaque bears the words "The Music Gallery referred to in the Rustall Manor Act of 1739". The building was moved to its present location from the other side of the Pantiles in 1850.

## 6.    Old Fish Market

There has been a fish market here since at least 1745 but the single-storey, black and white building now existing dates from around 1890. In the early 2000s it was the Tourist Information Centre but is now a dining venue.

## 7.    The Bath House

In front of the elegant frontage of the bath house built in 1804 are steps leading down to two glass-covered access points for the original chalybeate spring discovered around 1606 by Lord North. He had the red, scummy waters tested by his physician and declared to have health-giving properties. Taking the waters became popular with nobility and royalty and the buildings eventually erected to accommodate visitors grew into the town you now see before you. The prefix "Royal" was given by Edward VII in 1909 but by then the attractions of sea-bathing had led to decline in the popularity of the town as a resort and it was becoming a primarily residential development.

### Rustall Manor Act of 1739

The Pantiles was built by the Lord of the Manor on part of Tunbridge Wells Common and this clearly infringed the rights of those who had grazing and other rights on the Common (the "Freeholders"). When the Pantiles was built in the 1680s it was agreed that the Freeholders should be compensated by an annual payment but by 1732 this agreement had expired and the Freeholders were seeking further compensation. An agreement was negotiated that secured both the protection of the Common against further encroachment and the continued ownership of most of the Pantiles by the Lord of the Manor. This agreement was legislated as the Rustall Manor Act of 1739.

Leave the Pantiles and cross Neville Street to a small alleyway opposite. Pass one set of steps on the left and go up the second into Cumberland Gardens. Emerge into Mount Sion.

## 8.    Henry Fowler

Just before turning right up Mount Sion, glance across the road and to your left where there is a maroon plaque to Henry Fowler, famous as the author of Modern English Usage which was published in 1926 and, updated by Sir Ernest

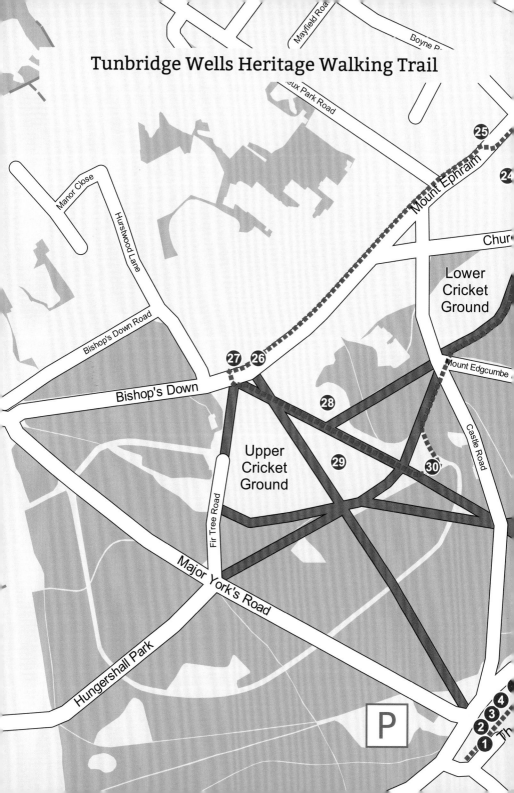

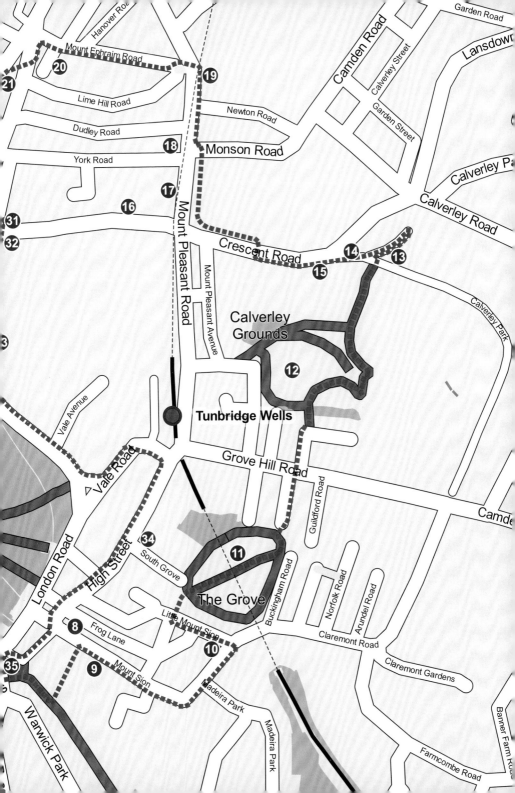

Gowers and Robert Burchfield, has been in print ever since. Fowler lived in Tunbridge Wells only as a child, his father being a teacher at Tonbridge School.

## 9. Jerningham House

Turn right uphill from Cumberland Gardens. The first house on the right is tile-clad Jerningham House, said to be one of the earliest lodging houses in Tunbridge Wells and dated in sales particulars to 1672. However, its Grade II listing dates it to 1746, which doesn't really fit.

Continue uphill, following Mount Sion round to the left at the top.

## 10.    63A Mount Sion

This modest house was occupied by Richard Cumberland (1732 to 1811), a prolific novelist and dramatist. His early career was as a civil servant, during which he was sent on a secret mission to negotiate a peace agreement with Spain during the American Civil War. The mission failed because of disagreement over Gibraltar. Cumberland retired to Tunbridge Wells for his second career, as Arthur Mee puts it in *The King's England*, "to write farces and tragedies, poems and novels, all poor and all forgotten".

*From an engraving by Hopwood after a painting by*
RICHARD CUMBERLAND (b. 1732, d.

Turn left down Little Mount Sion then right along Belgrove to...

The Grove

## 11.    The Grove

Mount Sion was owned by Viscountess Purbeck when in 1684 she realised its potential for development in the light of the growing number of people visiting the spring and began selling off plots for lodging houses and other facilities. Her son, the Duke of Buckingham, placed this land, then a small wood, in trust for the use of all inhabitants. The park suffered badly in army hands in World War II and lost many trees in the Great Storm of 1987 but has been replanted and is now a lively and attractive open space.

Go diagonally across The Grove, leave along Meadow Hill Road, cross Grove Hill Road and go down Mountfield Gardens into Calverley Grounds.

## 12. Calverley Grounds

The park was originally part of the estate laid out by Decimus Burton in the 1830s that included Calverley Park and the Calverley Hotel. Originally private grounds they became a public park in the 1920s. There are toilets and a café.

Cross the valley within the Grounds and take the path climbing out on the far side, keeping to the right of the café. On reaching Calverley Park go straight ahead to the first house on the right.

## 13.1 Calverley Park

Here lived Lord Dowding until his death in 1970. He served in the RAF and its predecessor organisations in both World Wars and as Air Chief Marshall is credited with Britain's success in the Battle of Britain. After retirement he took an interest in spiritualism, reincarnation and fairies.

Retrace your steps to the entrance to Calverley Grounds and turn right to a stone archway.

Calverley Grounds

## 14. Victoria Lodge

Like the rest of the Calverley estate, this sandstone gate is the work of architect Decimus Burton (see page 78).

Through the arch, bear left along Crescent Road passing…

## 15. Hotel du Vin & Bistro

Originally built as Calverley House in 1820, the building was enlarged by Decimus Burton in 1840 and became the Calverley Hotel. The Duchess of Kent and Princess Victoria stayed here when the house was Calverley House in 1827 and 1834.

At the crossroads, note ahead the spire of…

## 16. Holy Trinity Church

This Gothic revival church was designed by Decimus Burton at the western end of his Calverley estate but the linking buildings were demolished to make way for the civic centre in the 20th century. The building became "redundant for pastoral needs" in 1974 and is now the Trinity Theatre.

## 17. Canon Edward Hoare (1812 to 1894)

A member of the Hoare banking family, he was also the nephew of the prison reformer Elizabeth Fry, who was his mother's sister. Although his mother came from a Quaker family, he became a prominent member of the evangelical wing of the Church of England and wrote several books on religious themes. From 1853 until his death he was vicar of Holy Trinity Church and a leading figure in religious life in Tunbridge Wells.

Turn right along Mount Pleasant Road past the council offices. Down Monson Road on the right used to be the **museum** and **art gallery**. They have now been closed and at the time of writing are being redeveloped. The plan is to reopen the building in 2022 as **"The Amelia"**, named after the suffragist and Tunbridge Wells resident Amelia Scott. The official word is that this will be a "new and exciting Cultural and Learning space" that brings "together books, objects, documents, photographs, and visual art, housed in a vibrant and revitalised building".

## 18. Congregational Church

Opposite Monson Road and built by local stonemason Jabez Scholes between 1845 and 1848, the fine Tuscan portico was added in 1866. It is now a shop (Cotswold at the time of writing but it was formerly Habitat).

Continue along Mount Pleasant Road, passing on the right...

## 19. Opera House

The green-domed building was completed in 1902 and by 1931 had been turned into a cinema. It is now a Weatherspoon's pub but occasional operatic performances are held there.

At a paved area on the left, cross and bear right into Mount Ephraim Road. At the end, on the left corner, note...

## 20. Thackeray's

Dating from 1746 and originally known as Rock Villa, here William Makepeace

W M Thackeray

Thackeray, author of *Vanity Fair*, stayed in 1860 and wrote *Tunbridge Toys* for the *Cornhill Magazine* about the perils of getting into debt. He had previously set part of his novel The Virginians in Tunbridge Wells with which he was familiar from childhood visits.

Bear left along path across grassy area, cross London Road and continue uphill, passing on your left...

## 21. Belleville

This is where Thackeray stayed as a boy, easily viewed from the window of Rock Villa. Why he stayed here isn't clear but he was born in India in 1811 and sent to England without his mother in 1815 when his father died to be educated at various public schools – perhaps he spent the school holidays here. Certainly Belleville was a lodging house in 1881 when the census shows that it was run by a 49 year old Scottish widow with two pre-teen sons and a 62 year old married couple, the man being described as "Clergyman without care of souls".

Turn left along Mount Ephraim noting across the road the...

## 22. Royal Wells Hotel

Built in 1834 as the Mount Ephraim Hotel and then renowned for its views, the hotel has been adorned with the Royal coat of arms since 1840 and acquired its front bays and domed glass verandah later in the 19th century.

Next on the left is...

## 23. St Helena

This white cottage with tall brick chimneys bears a plaque marking it as the birth place of Frank Stone in 1841. By 1882 the cottage had presumably changed hands and Stone had become a local solicitor. The new owners obtained permission from the Committee managing the commons to enclose part of the common around the cottage within an iron fence for their use. Stone and his brother were livid at the Committee's lax approach to protecting the common from encroachment and recruited sixteen like-minded people to take over the Committee amid much furore. They were successful and able to bring about the return of a much stricter policy to encroachment.

Next on the left is…

## 24. Gibraltar Cottage

No house could be closer to the rocks than this, designed by Decimus Burton and built around 1828 on the site of a cottage dating back to 1700.

Cross Mount Ephraim and continue past number 66…

Gibraltar Cottage

## 25. Mayo House

Although the claret plaque mentions only John Mayo (1761-1818), his son Thomas (1790-1871) who took over the Tunbridge Wells practice in 1818 was probably the more eminent physician.

Continue along Mount Ephraim past the Travelodge (formerly the Wellington Hotel) to number 86…

## 26. The Chalet

This long, white building was the workshop of Edmund Nye and Thomas Barton who were manufacturers of Tunbridge ware which was decoratively inlaid woodwork, commonly boxes, often depicting local scenes and sold to visitors as souvenirs.

Next door is…

## 27. Mount Ephraim House

The original house on this site dates from around 1660, built by Sir Edmund King, physician to Charles II. He brought the Queen, Catharine of Braganza, to stay here in 1663, hoping that taking the waters would improve her health and perhaps help her to bear a son, although the King's frequent trips back to London to visit his mistress cannot h

achieve the latter. The house was extensively remodelled in the 19th century and while the Stewart character was retained it is not clear how much if any of the brickwork is original. The building is now a care home having recently undergone another major refurbishment.

Tunbridge Ware Box

Cross at the zebra crossing and take the path bearing left across the common, passing…

## 28. Wellington Rocks

One of the many fine outcrops of Ardingly sandstone in the Tunbridge Wells area – see page 7.

Wellington Roc...

## 29. The Common

The Common is one of the highlights of Tunbridge Wells, long used for leisure purposes including cricket and at one time there was a racecourse here. Since the cessation of grazing by sheep between the wars, the common has become more wooded and is now being managed to halt and even reverse the spread of scrub and woodland.

Continue along the hard path until you reach an avenue of trees.

## 30. Victoria Grove

Princess Victoria arrived in Tunbridge Wells on 5 August 1834 with her mother the Duchess of Kent and a large entourage. They stayed for nearly three months and in honour of the visit the people of the town planted this avenue of 132 elms, limes and sycamores in three rows twelve feet apart.

Most of the grove is on the right but to continue the trail turn left along the grove and at the end bear left to a track, along which turn right to the junction of Castle Road and Mount Edgcumbe Road. Cross to a path along the edge of Lower Cricket Ground and follow to crossroads. Cross carefully to opposite corner then cross grass to Inner London Road. Here is Ashton Lodge, also known as…

## 31. 69 London Road

Here lived Thomas Bayes from around 1734 to his death in 1761. He was minister of the Mount Sion chapel until 1752 but his fame arises from his work as a mathematician, particularly in the field of statistics. Bayesian techniques have become all the rage since the advent of electronic computers since they often require more computations than were hitherto feasible. These techniques have applications in fields such as drug trials where early results can be used to modify later stages in a trial to optimise the balance between gaining more information and avoiding unsuccessful treatments.

Head downhill across Church Road to the house on the corner…

69 London Road

## 32. Jordan House, 68 London Road

Here Humphrey Burrows Snr and Humphrey Burrows Jnr lived and made Tunbridge ware in the first half of the nineteenth century.

Continue down Inner London Road.

## 33. Vale Towers, 58 London Road

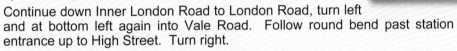

Rose Hill School once occupied Vale Towers, a Grade II listed "gothic" style building. Originally called Romonoff House School, it was founded in 1832 by Thomas Allfree who had been English tutor to the Russian Imperial household. He built Vale Towers from local stone in rather irregular gothic style in 1852 to accommodate the school. Robert Baden-Powell, founder of the Scout movement, attended the school from 1868 to 1870 before winning a scholarship to Charterhouse and continued to support the school later in life. The school now operates in premises on the northern edge of the town.

Baden-Powell

Continue down Inner London Road to London Road, turn left and at bottom left again into Vale Road. Follow round bend past station entrance up to High Street. Turn right.

## 34. High Street and Chapel Place

There are fine shop fronts in the High Street and some interesting goods to be viewed. When the High Street bears sharp right, go forward and cross the bottom of Mount Sion into brick-paved Chapel Place. This leads past more inviting shops, including a couple of second hand bookshops, to…

## 35. Church of King Charles the Martyr

The uninspiring brick exterior of this church belies the outstanding interior with gleaming white plasterwork that contrasts with the wooden pews and galleries. Originally a modest chapel built in 1676-84 to meet the needs of the visitors taking the waters, it was doubled in size in 1688-96 to meet the needs of a growing town. The elaborate stucco ceiling was by John Wetherill (first phase) and Henry Doogood who had worked for Sir Christopher Wren (second phase, partly to Wetherill's design).

There is a font of white Pentelic marble (from the quarries at Penteli north of Athens as was much of the marble used for the major monuments of classical Athens).

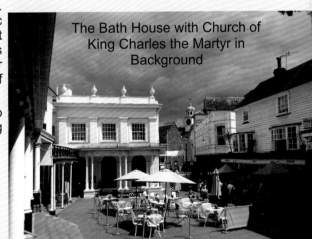

The Bath House with Church of King Charles the Martyr in Background

Cross Nevill Street to return to the Pantiles and your starting point.

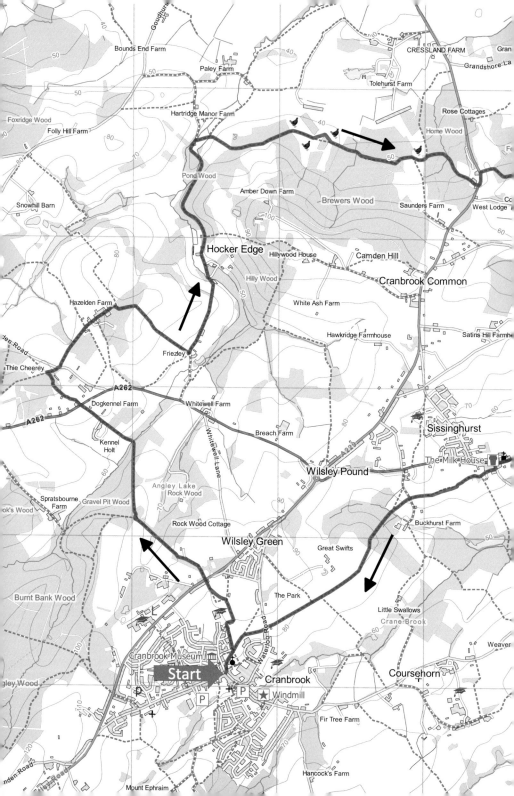

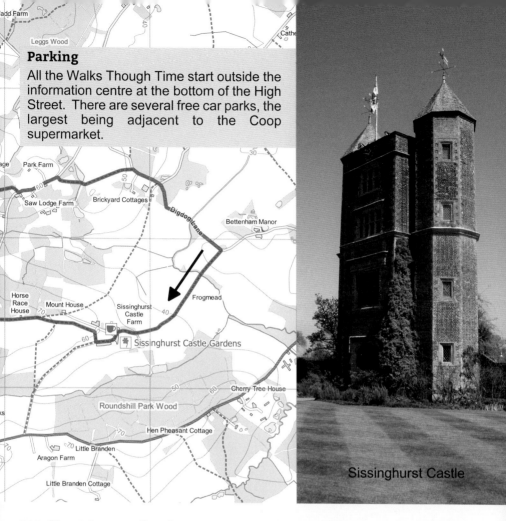

On the map: Jadd Farm, Leggs Wood, Cath..., age, Park Farm, Saw Lodge Farm, Brickyard Cottages, Digdog Lane, Bettenham Manor, Horse Race House, Mount House, Sissinghurst Castle Farm, Frogmead, Sissinghurst Castle Gardens, Cherry Tree House, Roundshill Park Wood, Hen Pheasant Cottage, Little Branden, Aragon Farm, Little Branden Cottage

**Parking**

All the Walks Though Time start outside the information centre at the bottom of the High Street. There are several free car parks, the largest being adjacent to the Coop supermarket.

Sissinghurst Castle

# Walks Through Time: Cranbrook and Sissinghurst (10.2 miles)

In front of information centre, go up steps into the churchyard of St Dunstan's and take path to left of church to top of churchyard. Bear left along a lane with buildings on your left and playground on your right. This becomes a footpath leading to a gate. Go through and just before larger gate straight ahead turn right along a path between hedge and fence. Follow path round a bend and out through a gate into a meadow. Bear left across the meadow down to a gate and along a track between fences to Angley Road, A229.

Take asphalt drive immediately opposite, through gate. Soon after left hand bend, go through a metal kissing gate on the left, through some trees and descend between fences to valley bottom. Climb the other side until just inside a wood there is a post bearing waymarks. Turn right through dilapidated gateway, soon descending through chestnut coppice to stream.

Cross, continue uphill to join asphalt drive past Kennel Holt and continue to main road, A262. Go straight across onto a path between fences. On reaching a drive, turn sharp right down to lane, Marden Road.

Bear right across lane to take track to Hazelden Farm. Go through farm and past various buildings until, by old hop pickers' huts on left, the path forks. Bear right into wood then left and right into open field. Head down grassy headland along left hand hedge of field to asphalt track at bottom. Turn left and follow track past delightful buildings in woodland valley. Keep going past Dene House, where the track becomes a path, and through woods eventually emerging alongside white weather boarded houses. After first house, bear right past second then take path through second gate on right.

Head diagonally across first field then up right hand side of next field into wood. Bear left through wood and emerge at fence surrounding free range chicken run. Go through metal gate and bear right, initially keeping to high ground and aiming for gap between two clumps of trees. Through gap, turn right downhill to gate in corner and go through. Follow path alongside fence (on your left) and just past corner enter woodland through another metal gate. Follow track to next metal gate, exit the enclosure again and take track ahead. After 60 metres bear left from broad track onto narrower path then bear left again on meeting another broad track. Bear right close to edge of wood (with field on right) and emerge by metal fence around another chicken run. Keep fence on your left and at corner go straight ahead into wood. Ignore

right turn after 100 metres but almost immediately follow main track around to right. When after another 50 metres the main track goes left, go straight ahead on path past green steel container. Keep going as path becomes a track and continue to main road, A229.

Cross carefully and turn left for 90 metres to lay-by and take path on right, soon entering woodland. Keep right at fork and right at next junction, climbing to edge of wood then over stile and along path between fences. Enter scrubby area and bear left then right to join lane near house.

Turn left along lane and after 300 metres take path over stile by gate on right. Bear left along track between fence and hedge to pond. Bear left up bank, out into field and straight across to kissing gate. Continue across next field to lane. Turn right and at junction go straight forward along Digdog Lane. After a gentle ascent, just before corner take track on right across fields with Elizabethan towers at Sissinghurst Castle soon coming into view. Just past the lowest point of the track, note Frogmead on your left.

On reaching National Trust property at Sissinghurst Castle, pass the garden on your left then turn left past entrance to garden and follow asphalt track round to right. On reaching entrance to car park, enter and follow path through car park to furthest point from entrance. Go through gap in fence at corner and along right hand edge of orchard to gap in fence leading onto stony track.

Bear left along track soon passing Horse Race House on your right. On reaching lane, turn sharp left over stile by gate into orchard. Go down obvious track until you reach a tree and a hedge on the left. Here bear half right along narrow path through apple trees towards far right corner. At corner, cross footbridge and head up left hand side of orchard to track. Turn right and follow track to main road (A262) at Sissinghurst.

Turn right and soon after church on right go down Chapel Lane on left. After 40 metres take path along track on right soon becoming narrow path between fences. At broad track go straight across and soon emerge along right hand edge of large field. Descend steps to lane, climb steps opposite into large steep field and descend to kissing gate at bottom. Go uphill through woodland and at gate bear right along concrete track. Follow all the way to road, cross and follow bottom of playing field to church. Go through churchyard to bottom corner and down steps to High Street.

# Points of Interest

## Cranbrook

The town, sometimes known as the capital of the Kentish Weald, was once the centre of clothmaking in Kent. In the 14th century Edward III invited Flemish weavers from Louvain to settle here and enable England to become self-sufficient in clothmaking rather than exporting most of its wool to be woven elsewhere. The industry thrived until the 17th century and died out in the early part of the 19th.

## Hazelden Farm

This group of buildings – incorporating Hazelden and Steddenden farmsteads, both listed buildings dating back to the 16th century – aligned along a track known as the Drift is a rare surviving example of traditional Wealden features. The Oast House is said to date from the 17th century. An archaeological survey in 2009, however, failed to find any prehistoric, Roman, Saxon or medieval artefacts. The hoppers' huts would have been used in the late 19th and 20th centuries prior to 1960 for Londoners who would come down in the late summer and autumn for a "holiday" picking hops.

## Friezley House

This timber framed house dates from 1608 when it was built by the Hovenden family whose wealth came from the cloth trade. It is "close studded" which means that the vertical timber struts are closer together and more numerous than the structure requires, their purpose being simply a show of wealth. It is now divided into two houses – Friezley and Weavers.

Cranbrook

## Hocker Edge

There has long been a water mill here, perhaps for as long as 500 years and formerly known as Hockridge Mill, which ground corn. It was owned by the

Hockridge Mill

Hovenden family from 1551 until at least 1704 and was the last water mill in Cranbrook parish to operate. At the lowest point of the track you can clearly see the structures for controlling the flow of water past the mill in the valley below. In the early 20th century Colonel Charles Grey lived here. In 1913 he moved into nearby Hartridge House which he had built in gardens that he had already created. After the First World War he moved north to help create the Royal Horticultural Society's Harlow Carr Garden. On returning, having sold Hartridge House, he moved back into the mill and created a new garden and a commercial nursery.

## Digdog Lane

The buildings on your right as you approach the junction were a brickworks for at least a century until 1970. Many of the houses in nearby Frittenden are built with bricks produced here. The name is said to have come from the medieval practice of burying the bodies of plague victims here, only to be dug up by dogs.

## Frogmead

This marshy area is being restored to the flood plain meadow that it once was when its long-gone frogs became acknowledged in its name. Hollows have been dug into which water will be diverted from the nearby stream, thus slowing the flow into rivers and hence reducing flood risk and soil erosion. The changed ecology should increase wildlife diversity including wetland birds, dragonflies and perhaps even frogs.

## Sissinghurst Castle

The castle was built by Sir John Baker and consisted of a large mansion around three courtyards. After housing French prisoners during the Seven Years War

Sissinghurst Castle

(1756-63), most of the buildings were demolished leaving the splendid gatehouse and parts of two wings converted into cottages. Harold Nicolson and his wife Vita Sackville-West bought the property in 1930 and created the celebrated garden now in the hands of the National Trust.

## Sissinghurst Village

Until the 1850s the village was known as Mylkhouse Street and had gained a poor reputation thanks to the smuggling activities of the Hawkhust Gang. The village pub, previously The Bull, is now called The Milk House.

## Great Swifts or Oak Hill Manor

There has been a house on this site at least since the 15th century when a dwelling was sold by a Stephen Swift. This presumably accounts for the various names of the house and the estate incorporating the name "Swift" or "Swifts". From 1789 to 1820 the house was owned by Major John Austen and his family, relatives of Jane Austen. The present house was built in 1938 by Major Victor Cazalet, MP for Chippenham, whose goddaughter, the actress Elizabeth Taylor, used to stay on the estate regularly as a child. He died in an air crash in 1943 after which the house was first let and then sold to the exiled Queen Maria of Yugoslavia and her sons. The house was renamed "Oak Hill Manor" in 1995 (and is still so named on current Ordnance Survey maps) but

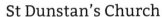

it has subsequently reverted to the former name of "Great Swifts".

## St Dunstan's Church

Records suggest that a church was first built on the current site in the early 1030s, probably a wooden structure named after St Dunstan, England's most popular saint.

St Dunstan was a 10th century English churchman who became both Archbishop of Canterbury and chief advisor to English kings, particularly King Edgar who ruled from 959 to 975 and was known as Edgar the Peaceful. Dunstan has been credited with the tradition of protecting a house by placing a horseshoe over the door. He was supposedly asked to re-shoe the Devil's cloven hoof but instead nailed a horseshoe to it causing such pain that in return for its removal the Devil undertook never to enter a house with a horseshoe above the door.

The huge and magnificent stone church, nicknamed "Cathedral of the Weald", owes its construction in the 15th and early 16th centuries to the prosperity resulting from the cloth trade. A notable feature is a figure of Father Time and his scythe above the clock face on the tower – the original wooden version is now in Cranbrook Museum, replaced on the tower in 1922 by one of stone with a real scythe covered in copper. Internally the church is light and airy with prominent memorials to the Roberts family of Glassenbury, including a large family tree engraved in marble. There are fine stained glass windows, some illustrated here.

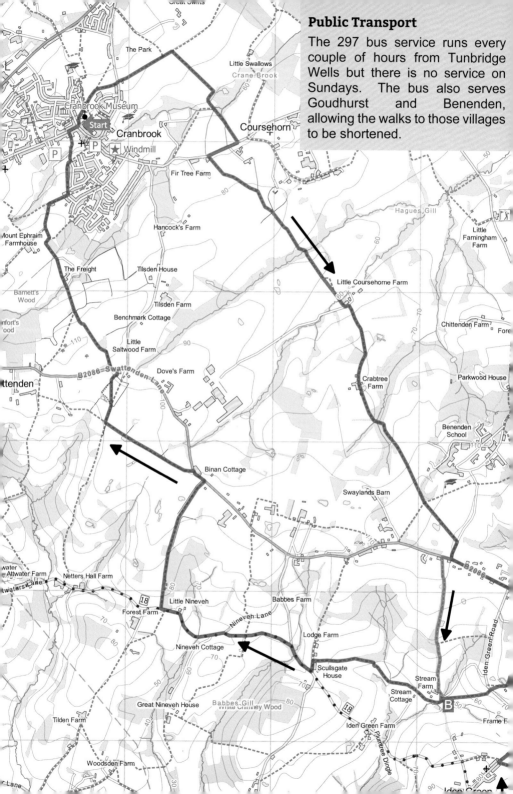

**Public Transport**

The 297 bus service runs every couple of hours from Tunbridge Wells but there is no service on Sundays. The bus also serves Goudhurst and Benenden, allowing the walks to those villages to be shortened.

# Walks through Time: Cranbrook and Benenden (10.9, 8.5 or 8.0 miles)

The first half of the walk, from Cranbrook to the entrance to Benenden School, follows the High Weald Landscape Trail which is waymarked with appropriate stickers.

In front of information centre, go up steps into churchyard of St Dunstan's and follow path to the left of the church to the top. Keep right between playground on left and hedge on right. Continue along bottom edge of recreation ground and down steps to Waterloo Road.

Take footpath immediately opposite, up steps, initially between fences but soon with fence only on left. At start of a concrete section of path turn sharp right down left hand side of field. At bottom of field, turn right and follow edge of woodland then at waymark post turn sharp left downhill to a footbridge. Across the bridge, follow left hand edge of field to first corner, then pass through gap, over stream and across field to Golford Road.

Turn right and follow road carefully for just over 200 metres then take path between fences alongside drive. At stile go through hedge and follow right hand edge of a couple of fields. Bear half right across next field, making for gate. Follow left hand edge of next field and go through kissing gate beside second field gate in hedge on left to follow instead right hand edge of adjacent field. At corner go over stile and down steps into Wealden ghyll. Bear left across footbridge and up other side to emerge in field. Follow right hand edge of field until it

turns right, then go straight across the field to a footbridge in woodland at the bottom. Across the bridge, climb bank, keeping to the right of the large animal shed. Turn left along the track then turn right uphill along farm track.

Follow track to Crabtree Farm. When the track forks in front of the farmhouse, take the left fork along the left hand side of a hedge. Beyond the farm, cross a field and enter woodland. Cross bridge over stream and follow fence uphill to corner then bear right along top edge of wood. Emerge along a path initially parallel to the edge of the wood but soon bearing left uphill to the corner of the field. From the corner, bear left towards a gate into a playing field belonging to Benenden School. Bear left along the field edge to another gate. Continue forward across parkland with fence on right and at school driveway turn right down to road.

*For short walk, follow the instructions for Link Route 1 and resume at Point B below.*

*For long and medium walks, turn left and follow road through Benenden to the large village green on the right. Go up the lane to the right of the green to the church at the top.*

*For medium walk, follow the instructions for Link Route 2 and resume at Point A below.*

*For long walk, enter the churchyard and bear left along path into field. Follow right hand edge of field then pass new school on left to junction with High Weald Landscape Trail. Turn right along the trail and on reaching track turn right for a short distance then go through gate on left. Bear gradually away from left hand edge of field, heading downhill towards wood. Follow path through wood to*

Strawberry Wood Culvert with information board. Emerge into field and follow clear HWLT waymarks alongside and through woodland to lane.

Turn right and follow lane to The Woodcock public house. Just before the pub, take path on right along concrete track past sewage works and then cross orchard to far side. Turn left along path to lane at Iden Green. Turn right and at first bend take path on right diagonally across field to group of large trees. Go forward along farm driveway and at first bend take path on left along edge of orchard, across another drive, past a house and on entering field turn right along track. Follow track along right hand edge of field then between hedges alongside churchyard to stile on left at junction of paths.

This is **Point A** where Link Route 2 from the village green at Benenden joins the main route.

Go over stile and diagonally across field to stile in hedge. Continue in same direction to stile beside field gate at corner and then down to stile in fence. Cross Iden Green Road very carefully and take path through hedge opposite. Follow path downhill with hedge on left to meet track leading to Stream Farm.

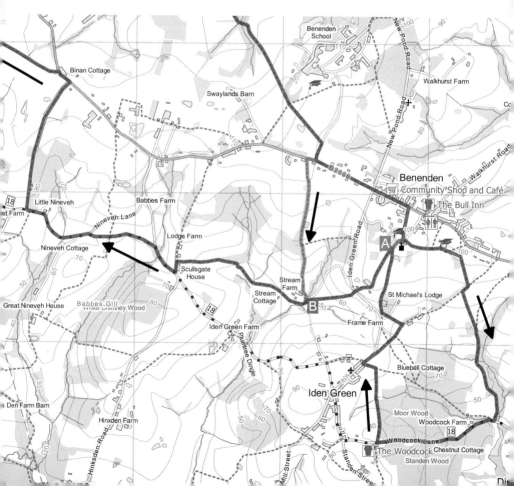

This is **Point B** where Link Route 1 from the entrance to Benenden School joins the main route.

In front of farm gate go down bank and through small gate. Cross footbridge, go over stile and along lower boundary of farm. At Stream Cottage turn right over stile then left along path between fences. Emerging into field, bear slightly right uphill across middle of field to stile. Cross bridge over ditch and make for far right corner of field. Follow path through several gates to T-junction then turn left past Scullsgate House to Babb's Lane (National Cycle Network Route 18).

Turn right along lane, keeping left at junctions until at a sharp left hand bend you pass Little Nineveh, a fine tile-hung farmhouse with a single oast house nearby. 150 metres past farm, take path on right up steps into wood. Continue through wood, along right hand side of field and halfway along (where the hedge line kinks) go through gate (without changing direction) to follow left hand side of second field, then between fences to Cranbrook Road, B2086.

Turn left and at first bend take path on left along left hand edges of two fields. Cross middle of next field to gap in hedge, go through and turn right uphill along field edge to stile. The path should now go diagonally left across field and through a couple of rows of apple trees but at the time of writing the trees are obstructing the path. To avoid the obstruction, follow the left hand edge of the next field to the corner and then turn right along the left hand edge of what is here an orchard (shown in red on the map) until you reach a stile on the left (or a gap if the stile is not repaired soon).

Over stile or through gap, follow right hand edge of another field to corner then turn left and continue along hedge until you reach a gap (which may be a little overgrown) into Swattenden Lane, B2086.

Cross carefully to path opposite, cross narrow strip of woodland and then follow right hand edge of field. Follow field edge as it weaves left and right, but when it turns sharp right go straight across field towards line of trees. Keep to left of these to field corner, go through a small copse and along left hand edge of next field and join a track that takes you past Bluebell Barn (with The Freight behind) on right. Continue along track as it becomes a lane and, after a right turn, pass row of cottages on right.

On meeting street (Bramley Drive), turn left and almost immediately take path on left enclosed by trees. At bottom, turn right then first left through play area, across stream and past car park to High Street. Turn right to return to starting point.

## Link Route 1

Emerging from the drive to Benenden School, turn right along road and after about 65 metres take path through wooden gate on left. Go along path between hedges for 300 metres or so then down right hand edge of field towards Stream Farm. This section of the path follows the course of a Roman road from Rochester to the south coast. At bottom, bear left through gate and down to farm track. Continue from Point B as above.

## Link Route 2

Turn right along asphalt track in front of church and follow round to left to junction of tracks and stile.

# Points of Interest

## Coursehorne

This small hamlet includes half a dozen listed buildings including an old cloth house, a large barn and an oast house. Only the barn can be clearly seen from the route but Dulwich Preparatory School occupies the main house and during term time the chatter of children can often be heard. The Dulwich College Preparatory School in London was briefly evacuated here in 1939 before a further move to Betws-y-Coed but there is no indication on their web sites that the schools are currently connected.

## Crabtree House

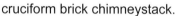
Crabtree House

Originally a 16th century timber-framed house. The tiles hung on the upper storey and the brickwork encasing the lower storey were added later. It was probably re-roofed in 1729 and may previously have been thatched. In the centre of the roof is a late 16th century cruciform brick chimneystack.

Benenden School

## Benenden School

Then called Hemsted Park, the mansion at the heart of the school was completed in 1862 for owner Lord Cranbrook. It was substantially remodelled into a Tudor-cum-Jacobean style in 1912 after acquisition by Sir Harold Harmsworth, later Lord Rothermere, a press magnate particularly associated with the *Daily Mail* and the *Daily Mirror*. The school moved here in 1924 and now educates over 500 girls, all boarders.

## Benenden

This very attractive village owes much to the endeavours of Lord Cranbrook who lived at Hemsted Park from 1862 until his death in 1906. He refurbished the church, although in a style currently out of fashion, and had buildings removed to create the splendid green now at the centre of the village and accommodate a cricket pitch. On the west side of the green he had a school built for infants and older girls to complement the pre-existing Gibbon School for boys on the northern side (founded in James I's reign by a member of the family to which historian Edmund Gibbon belonged and still bearing his name today). The elegant former building remained in use as a primary school until

September 2019 when a new building was opened to the east of the village hall.

Benenden was once the home of Marion Cran, the first person to broadcast on gardening in Britain in the 1920s and a breeder and judge of pedigree cats. She was immortalised in a comic rhyme by Reginald Arkell in 1934:

> Beverley Nicholls and Marion Cran
> Hadn't been born when the world began
> That is the reason I must confess
> Why the Garden of Eden was not a success

## Strawberry Wood Culvert

Strawberry Wood is ancient woodland typical of the High Weald. The sweet chestnut and hornbeam trees have long been coppiced, that is cut down to near ground level every ten to fifteen years and allowed to re-grow. The harvested wood may traditionally have been used in ships or buildings or to make charcoal but in more recent times for fencing.

The age of the culvert, a very strong stone structure that carried a track over a stream, is not known. It had been severely damaged by flood water and was restored in 2009 using local stone. Theories as to its original purpose include transportation of iron ore in Tudor times or the carrying of cloth to and from a fulling mill during the heyday of the Wealden cloth industry – see page 60.

## Stream Farm and Paved Roman Ford

As you pass the southern boundary of the farm you are close to the site of a paved ford where a Roman road from Rochester crossed the stream. Fords were a common feature of Roman roads but few survive in Britain, although more have done so elsewhere in the former Roman Empire. The Historic England web site claims that the site "survives comparatively well"; on the other hand Peter Brandon in his book *The Kent and Sussex Weald* reports that it "was destroyed in the exceptional floods in the autumn of 2000". While the remains of the ford are not now obvious, it is possible from the path to spot a triangular boundary stone later inserted into the ford. The stone marks the meeting point of three Kent hundreds, the seventy or so administrative units into which the county was divided from Saxon times until 1892. There are inscriptions on at least two and probably all of the three faces of the stone, presumably the names of the three hundreds, Cranbrook, Selbrittenden and Rolvenden.

## Scullsgate House

Formerly Scullsgate Farmhouse, this 17th century or earlier timber-framed building is largely hung with tiles.

## Little Nineveh

No one now knows for sure why this farm and nearby Great Nineveh are named after the capital of the ancient Assyrian

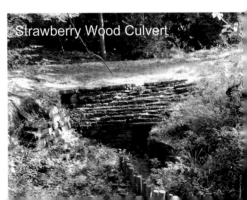
Strawberry Wood Culvert

empire. It has been suggested that the properties may have been owned by Dissenters, Protestant Christians who separated from the Church of England in the 17th and 18th centuries, although it is not obvious why they would have wanted to name their farms after a city described in the Bible as wicked and worthy of destruction.

## The Freight

The timber-framed building, ground floor clad in brick and first floor hung with tiles, is a 15th century former cloth hall. Beside the stream below the house there may have been a fulling mill, not used since the end of the 16th century.

# The Wealden Wool Industry

During the 16th and 17th centuries the Weald was one of Britain's most industrialised areas, dominated by the production of woollen textiles and iron. There were two chief woollen products – broadcloth and kersey. The production of the cheaper kersey cloth took place on the north-eastern edge of the Weald and in villages on and around the Greensand ridge such as Egerton and Pluckley.

The broadcloth industry was concentrated in an area around Cranbrook – the majority of those involved lived in the parishes of Cranbrook, Biddenden, Benenden, Goudhurst, Hawkhurst, Smarden, Staplehurst and Horsmonden. A piece of Kent broadcloth had to be about a metre wide, at least 28 yards long and at least 86 pounds in weight.

The industry was organised by clothiers who contracted out the various steps in the process to subcontractors. They would obtain the wool, perhaps from the sheep of Romney Marsh. Kentish broadcloth was "dyed in the wool", that is the wool was dyed before weaving rather than the cloth being dyed afterwards. This was usually done on the clothier's premises using a combination of red dyes (madder, brazil and cochineal) and blue dyes (woad, copperas and indigo) to produce a range of colours.

The dyed wool was then distributed to spinners, usually working in their own homes. It would take a day to spin a pound of wool.

The spun wool was then distributed to the weavers who owned their own looms, often accommodated in large halls that characterise their houses which remain part of the Weald's fine architectural heritage. Looms were not expensive so it was relatively easy to set up as an independent weaver.

The next stage was fulling. Unlike the preceding stages of production, this process required heavy investment in a dedicated building and specialised machinery – a fulling mill. Fuller's earth would be applied to the cloth and a water-powered hammer would beat the cloth to remove grease and smooth the cloth. There were only a dozen or so fulling mills serving hundreds of clothiers and thousands of spinners and weavers so a significant amount of movement of heavy pieces of cloth was required.

After fulling, the cloth was washed and stretched to dry on wooden frames, held in place by tenterhooks. Finally the cloth was "dressed" by shearmen who would raise the nap by passing teasels across the cloth then clip off the raised fibres with shears.

The wool industry brought much wealth to Cranbrook and the surrounding area. Authorities differ on the reason for its demise in the late 17th century. Some claim it was the belated result of the introduction under Elizabeth I of a ban on the export of cloth for dying and finishing in Flanders but broadcloth was dyed before weaving so that makes little sense. More likely the clothiers responded to changing markets by moving their capital into other lines of business, especially agriculture, as they had always had diverse commercial interests, so that by the early 18th century it was history. The iron industry was gone too so that the Weald became one of the few areas to deindustrialise, allowing the landscape to develop the exceptional scenery that walkers are now free to enjoy.

# The Culpeper Family

For many people the name Culpeper is primarily associated with the book *The Complete Herbal* which describes the medicinal uses of hundreds of plants. However, Nicholas Culpeper who wrote the book was born in Surrey, raised in Sussex and practised mainly in London. The Kent Culpepers were more interested in industry and commerce, from which they became very wealthy. Bedgebury Manor passed into the family's hands in 1425 when Walter Culpeper married the widow of John Bedgebury; there it remained for 250 years. Their grandson Sir Alexander Culpeper benefited from the iron foundries on the estate which were used to cast guns for the fleet that fought the Spanish Armada. This is the family so many of whose members are the subject of superb memorials in Goudhurst church. Thomas Culpeper who was executed by Henry VIII for his relationship with Catherine Howard is also related to this family.

There were also wealthy Culpepers in Sussex, particularly Sir Edward Culpeper of Wakehurst Place (now a National Trust property and home to the national seed bank) whose daughter Catherine married Richard Ifield of Gravetye Manor, later home of the eminent garden designer William Robinson.

Culpeper Tombs in Goudhurst Church

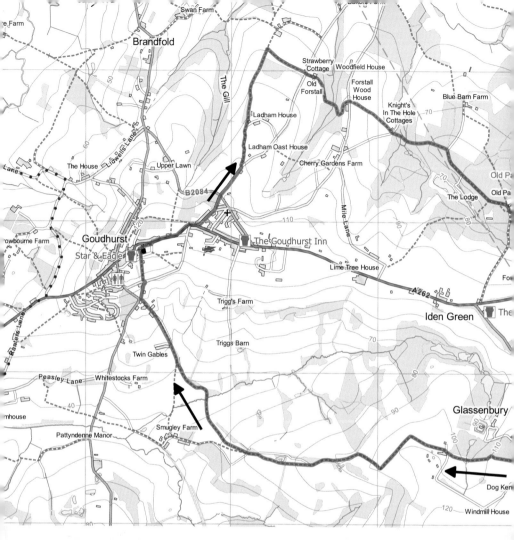

# Walks through Time: Cranbrook and Goudhurst (10.2 miles)

The first half of the walk, from Cranbrook to Goudhurst, follows the High Weald Landscape Trail which is waymarked with appropriate symbols (although there are gaps).

Start outside the information centre. Walk up High Street and after 640 metres turn right along New Road. At end cross Angley Road (A229) into Angley Wood. At highest point of track, take roughly parallel path on left (High Weald Landscape Trail). On reaching broad track, turn right then almost immediately left down path (WC90) through tall pines. At bottom bear left over small bridge along broad undulating track for 540 metres until immediately before it starts to turn consistently left uphill. Bear right along another broad track downhill to valley bottom. Take narrower path

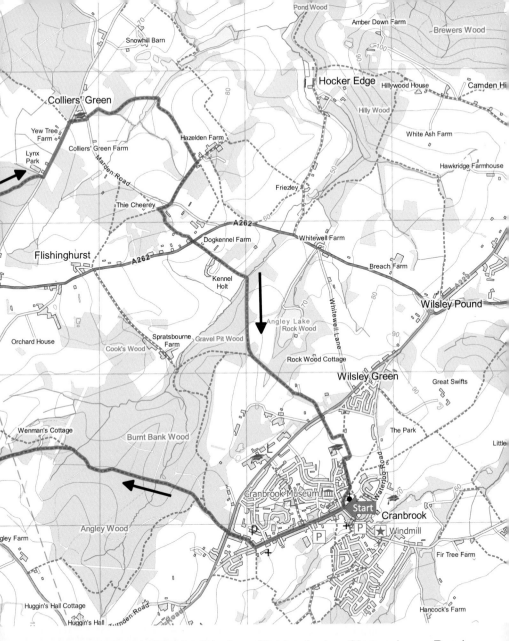

very slightly left of straight ahead, quite steeply uphill. On meeting concrete track at top, bear left along track and follow until it bears sharp left at farm. Take path on left just before the bend and follow, parallel with track to Glassenbury Road, B2085.

Go straight across and down right hand edge of field with glimpses of Glassenbury House through trees on right. At bottom cross bridge and climb up to meet drive at top. Go straight ahead along track, follow round sharp left turn along field edge then sharp right at corner. At next corner bear left past some ponds with fine views of Goudhurst on hill on right. Keep going in generally the same direction (most people follow the rough track although, strictly, the poorly waymarked path is sometimes a few tens of metres to the left). When track bends left between fields, take path on right down field to footbridge over ditch, across another track and go down field to footbridge over stream at bottom.

Follow path uphill along right hand side of field to track. Turn right and follow to junction with metalled drive leading to large houses on left. Take path just to left of drive ahead, running uphill parallel to drive and re-joining it at top. Follow drive uphill to Maypole Lane.

Turn right and at junction take footpath at top of the bank up steps then uphill into churchyard. Bear left to High Street where there are various opportunities for refreshment.

Head back uphill towards the church and go through the churchyard to the far left corner. Cross the road to the old weavers' cottages and continue east along the pavement round left and right hand bends.

Take the first left (Tattlebury Lane) downhill, keep left at junction and at crossroads go straight across along Ladham Road. Turn left down drive to Ladham House and when drive bears right take track on left between bollards. After 500 metres take path over stile in hedge on right and follow path across field and through orchard. At hedge go through gate and past garages to lane.

Bear right across lane down asphalt drive to Old Forstal and at end go straight ahead through hole in hedge into woodland. Bear right along track, at corner turning left downhill to plank bridge across stream. Bear right uphill then left past house and finally right again to Jarvis Lane.

Take path (WC18) opposite between fence and hedge then down through orchard edge to gate. Take path past house and bear left across track to metal pedestrian gate. Descend through woodland to footbridge across stream and continue uphill through woodland on the other side. At top join chalk track then bear right along asphalt/concrete track through wood to Old Park Cottage. Take first path on left past Cottage (WC21) and follow, going straight across at first junction and keeping right at fork, to reach lane at Lynx Park.

Turn left for 400 metres and take path on right over stile by a pair of gates. Cross school car park and scrub to another lane, turn left and very shortly take path (WC81A) on right initially along right hand edge of field. At first corner, enter wood and follow track to emerge into field at corner. Go straight across downhill between two lakes and up bank through hedge. Turn right, go through gap into next field and turn left uphill. Go straight across three fields to join track at Hazelden Farm. Turn right along track to lane (Marden Road).

Bear right across lane and up gravel track. Soon take path into wood on left heading away from track and continue to road, A262.

Go straight across down lane and keep going to footbridge at the bottom. Climb up through woodland until at top there is a fence ahead and fields beyond. Bear slightly left downhill with woodland on left and open fields on right. Pass lake on right and climb up to drive. Turn right and right again to Angley Road, A229.

Go straight across down narrow path between gardens to open meadow. Head up to top corner and then right along path between fences, bearing right and emerging by school. Turn sharp left down path towards Cranbrook church, enter churchyard and bear right to High Street.

# Points of Interest

## Glassenbury

The moated house can just be glimpsed through the trees from the public footpath, especially in winter when the trees are leafless. Although the house is said to date from the late 15th century, it has been substantially altered and remodelled. The house changed hands many times in the 20th century. Between the wars it was used as a school, from 1938 to 1940 to accommodate refugee children and during the last war it housed a military hospital. After later spells as a wedding venue, a location for films and television and a conference venue, Glassenbury is now a private home again.

Glassenbury

Writer Richard Church was particularly taken with Glassenbury's tapestry bedroom whose walls were "covered entirely in needlework done in blue and cream embroidery". Jaffa, one of Napoleon's horses, is buried in the garden. Authorities differ as to who brought the horse back from Waterloo – either it was "one of the sons of the house who was in Wellington's entourage" (Richard Church) or it was a Frenchman, once a great friend of Napoleon, to whom the house was then leased (the San Francisco Morning Call).

## Smugley Farm

This Grade 2 listed, timber-framed 16th century farmhouse sits close to the line of the former Hawkhurst branch line which was completed in 1892 and connected to the main railway network at Paddock Wood. Except in the hop-picking season when there were special trains bringing hop-pickers down from London, the line was never busy and no one was surprised when its closure was announced in 1961. There is talk of creating a walking and cycle track along all or part of the line, which would be a huge asset to the area. Some of the line is well preserved but there are also major issues with land ownership and obstruction by dwellings and businesses. One can only hope that these obstacles might be overcome.

# Goudhurst

Perched atop a ridge of Upper Tunbridge Wells sandstone, the village is visible from miles around and the top of the church tower affords unrivalled views of the surrounding Wealden countryside.

The village's prosperity came from the broadcloth and iron industries. The

Goudhurst

davidramshaw.co.uk

weavers' cottages across the road from the churchyard date from about 1350, soon after the arrival of Flemish weavers in Cranbrook and the spread of the cloth industry to the surrounding area.

There was an ironworks at nearby Bedgebury owned originally by Alexander Culpeper; the furnace pond can still be traced but the remains of the forge were largely destroyed when the Hawkhurst branch line was constructed.

The table-tomb bearing wooden effigies of Sir Alexander and Lady Constance Culpeper, with gesso detailing and colouring, is a remarkable feature of the interior of Goudhurst Church (see page 61).

Church House

## Rootes Motors

The Rootes motor manufacturing company, which included the Hillman, Humber and Sunbeam marques, was founded by brothers William and Reginald Rootes. Their interest in engineering can be traced back to their father's cycle sales and repair business which operated from the basement of Church House in Goudhurst High Street opposite the Star & Eagle in the late 1890s. Their father, inspired by David Salomons' first motor show in 1895, then moved into motor sales and servicing in Hawkhurst and Maidstone and this business was sold to the brothers who then expanded into motor manufacturing in 1929. In 1967 Rootes was in financial difficulties and was acquired by Chrysler, then sold on to Peugeot in 1978 and by 1981 was gone.

## The Hawkhurst Gang

A reign of terror by a group of smugglers known as the Hawkhurst Gang was brought to an end in Goudhurst on 21 April 1747. When the people of Goudhurst established a militia to defend against the smugglers, gang leader

Thomas Kingsmill who came from Goudhurst was so affronted that he announced his intention to attack the village. Forewarned, the village militia were ready for them and killed or captured many of the gang. Most of those captured were hanged, Kingsmill's body being brought back to Goudhurst and hung in chains at a road junction near Gore Court.

Star & Eagle

## Star & Eagle

Formerly called the Star and Crown, internally the building is old, perhaps 15th century, but externally the mock Tudor façade with its jetties, gables and gallery is entirely of 20th century construction. The current hotel is an amalgamation of three buildings – the original Inn, a building that was once Lloyds bank and a former inn, the Eight Bells. The Inn is reputedly connected to the church vaults by an underground passage that may have been used by the Hawkhurst Gang when operating from the Inn.

## The Vine

Situated at the crossroads by Goudhurst pond, The Vine was built in the early 17th century as a coaching inn and has a number of later additions. At first sight it appears to be clad in white weatherboarding like the Burgess Stores opposite. A closer examination shows that the upper storey of the front elevation is hung with clay tiles that have been rather spoiled by a coat of white paint. The Vine has changed hands and function rather frequently in recent years – at the time of writing it is a pub and restaurant.

The Vine

## Ladham House

The house was built in 1831 and substantially enlarged in the early 1860s. The fine garden and grounds are occasionally open under the National Garden Scheme.

## Angley Wood

The wood is so large that you pass through it near both the start and the end of the walk. The wooded parkland was described by Charles Igglesden, author of 34 volumes of *A Saunter through Kent with Pen and Pencil* (published from 1899 to 1944), as the most delightful in the country. The original estate has long ago been broken up and sold off. There have been various mansions within what was once a 334 hectare estate but they are long gone, replaced by a 1930s house of no particular distinction.

# Walks Through Time: Cranbrook and Bedgebury (12.8 or 9.8 miles)

From the information centre go up the High Street for 70 metres and take path on left immediately past Royal Mail depot. Keep to the left of the car park down to a footbridge over the River Crane. Across the bridge climb up to street, immediately turn right along drive and after just a few metres take enclosed path on left. On reaching street again, take first turn on right along the narrow Freight Lane (restricted byway). Keep left at unmarked junctions and, after 700 metres or so, pass Bluebell Barn on the left (with The Freight behind) and

descend to bridge. Go up right hand edge of meadow then through hedge into arable field. Bear right diagonally across field – aim to pass to right of pair of large oaks, one half dead and the other thriving, and left of electricity pole on the skyline. Maintain direction to reach Swattenden Lane at far corner.

Take footpath opposite and pass to left of pond. Bear right through fence and forward along enclosed track. On reaching open field, go straight down the middle, pass along left hand side of disconnected hedge and enter wood on right at bottom. Descend into wooded ghyll, cross footbridge over stream and climb out into field. Bear left across field and near end descend into another wooded ghyll on left. On the other side, head straight across

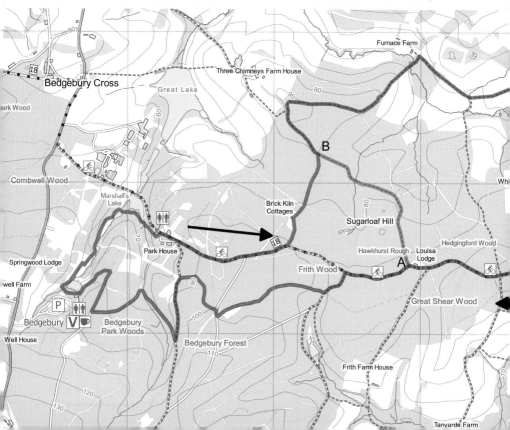

View from Visitor Centre, Bedgebury

field to projecting corner and field gate then head straight down field to pedestrian gate into another ghyll. On tar side follow left hand edge of first field and cross stream then bear right across next field to corner and into third field where there are outcrops of Ashdown sandstone. Keep left along path to Water Lane and turn left.

At road junction turn right along Potter's Lane. After 375 metres, just before lane crosses stream, take path (WC174) on right. Climb though trees into field and turn left along edge, re-entering wood on left through gate near corner. Cross stream and just before gate turn right along narrow strip of woodland for 100 metres then turn right again, back across stream. Head uphill through orchard; turn left at the top and follow track through farm to Water Lane. Turn left and follow to main road (A229).

Cross carefully to footway, turn left then after a few metres turn right along Park Lane. Follow lane for 650 metres to junction, keep right along asphalt track to pass Foresters Lodge and continue along stony track. Keep straight ahead until you reach Louisa Lodge on your right. This is point A on the map and here you can either

bear left to continue to Bedgebury Forest or bear right for the shortcut (orange route on map).

**If taking the shortcut**, bear right along the bridleway through the forest for 1.1 km to point B where you rejoin the main route and bear slightly right.

**If tackling the full route**, bear left along National Cycle Route 18 for 460 metres then take first left along bridleway. At Post 32 take first right along the blue family cycling route. At T-junction (Post 27) turn right then very shortly second left opposite Post 26. At next T-junction (Post 23) turn left uphill. At next junction (Post 20) double back downhill and at bottom turn left uphill on gravel track, now leaving the family cycle route (Post 16).

Pass Gruffalo on left and at junction at top turn right through gate along gravel track along ridge. Take the first gravel track on the left, doubling back downhill to visitor centre. Loop round the lake and head down the valley on the far side along an asphalt path. Pass two small lakes on right and immediately after the second turn right along path with much larger Marshall's Lake on your left. Cross footbridge at the end of the lake, turn right along path for a few metres then take path on left climbing steeply to toilets. Go through gate to right of toilets, go forward to track (National Cycle Route 18 again) and turn right

Keep left at all junctions and at fork bear left (leaving National Cycle Route 18). Pass Brick Kiln Cottages and keep going in roughly the same direction until you reach bridleway at Point B where the shortcut comes in from the right. Turn left.

Marshall's Lake, Bedgebury

For both routes, follow bridleway for 375 metres past junction on left. Continue round a sharp right hand bend and take right hand fork through woods. At crossways turn left and when track bears left go forward along bridleway, soon descending along a sunken track. At bottom cross bridge and at T junction turn right and follow bridleway to A229 at Hartley. If the timing is right you could skip the last 1.5 miles along the road by taking a bus from here into Cranbrook – the bus stop is just down the hill to the right. Otherwise cross the road carefully to the footway on the far side and turn left. Keep straight on at the junction with the B2086 and pass the Hartley Coffee Shop or drop in as you wish. On reaching a fork, bear right along the High Street and as you approach the town centre admire the very fine buildings on both sides of the road. You will soon be back at your starting point.

# Points of Interest

## Bedgebury National Pinetum and Forest

There are lakes, cycle routes, walking routes, a cafe and an adventure playground. There are miles of tracks for walking, cycling and horseriding. Entry is free if you don't come by car but parking is not cheap – check prices before you visit. There is also a Go Ape treetop adventure at additional cost.

## Bedgebury Park

The house was built in red brick in 1688 by James Hayes with the profits from the salvage of a sunken Spanish treasure ship. In 1836 the house was bought by William Carr Beresford and his wife Louisa after whom Louisa Lake and Louisa Lodge are named. He enlarged the house and encased it in sandstone ashlar so that it now rather resembles a French chateau.

The estate was bought by the government in 1919 for the Forestry Commission who in partnership with Kew Gardens undertook the relocation of Kew's conifer collection to Bedgebury. The partnership ended in 1965 when Kew Gardens decided to concentrate on developing Wakehurst Place in Sussex as their rural outpost. The great storm of 1987 destroyed a third of Bedgebury's tree collection. The development of cycling routes and an increased focus on adventurous days out began around 2005.

The house was not needed by the Forestry Commission and was sold to the Church Education Corporation who used it for a girls' boarding school from 1920 until 2006. The house is now occupied by the Bell Bedgebury International School.

## Furnace Farm

This is the site of the blast furnace that operated here in the days of the Wealden iron industry. In 1637 it was run by John Browne who also operated the Horsmonden furnace and held the post of King's Gunfounder. The remains of the nearby forge were destroyed when the Hawkhurst branch line was built. The dam (or "bay") of the pond that held water to power the iron works is still visible nearby although breached so that the pond is now drained.

# Walks Through Time: Cranbrook North (2.6 miles)

Start outside the information centre. Walk up High Street and after 640 metres turn right along New Road. Cross carefully and go into Angley Wood opposite. Initially follow the High Weald Landscape Trail but this soon leaves your route on the left. Follow the main track round to the right, pass a junction on the left and bear right into small clearing. On far side take right fork (with Angley Stud on the skyline over the fence on your right). Continue to avoid all left turns until you reach a waymarked junction and there is path ahead between fences. Here turn left downhill between high banks (or walk on the left bank above the path to avoid mud and, at the time of writing, a fallen tree near the bottom). Follow path round to the right, gradually descending to a metal structure on a bridge (to allow horses but not motor bikes to pass).

Over the bridge, take right fork down to concrete bridge, cross stream again and continue on a rising track bearing gently right. When the path starts to descend again, pass junction of paths and continue downhill between fences with paddocks and a small lake (sometimes dry) on your right. Past the lake, climb again to join drive and follow to Angley Road, A229.

Go straight across down narrow path between gardens to open meadow. Bear left to top corner and go along path between fences, bearing right and emerging by school. Turn left down path towards Cranbrook church, enter churchyard and bear right to High Street.

## Toilets

Cranbrook's main shortcoming at the time of writing is the lack of public toilets. Those previously available have been closed due to vandalism and are to be demolished. There are plans for a new community centre with toilets and meanwhile interim arrangements are being sought – perhaps they will be in place by the time of your visit.

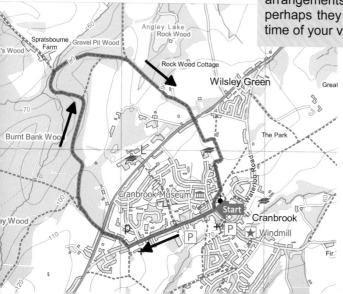

# Points of Interest

## Vestry Hall

Now housing the Weald Information Centre, the building was erected in 1859 to accommodate a courthouse on the first floor (the George Hotel having previously served this purpose) and the fire station on the ground floor.

## Cramp Institute Club

Now a social club, it was built as a Baptist Chapel in 1807. A guidebook of 1894-5 refers to it as "the Cramp Institute for lads and young men".

## Old Studio and Broadcloth Cottage

Opposite the Cramp Institute are three fine timber-framed cottages, probably built as a single Wealden Cloth Hall in the late 15th century and later subdivided. The one on the left, the Old Studio, was used by the Cranbrook Colony – see page 77.

## Spratsbourne Farm and Water Mill

In the mid 17th century the stream near Spratsbourne Farm was dammed to create Tucker's pond to feed a mill which had already been operating for some time, perhaps since the 14th century. The pond regularly froze in winter and was used by the townsfolk for skating; the area became known as Little Switzerland. Although the mill is known as a corn mill, "tucker" is an old word for a fuller and it may be that at one time it was a fulling mill (see page 60). Both Spratsbourne Mill and Hockeredge Mill (see Sissinghurst walk) were operated by the Bonnick family, in particular William Bonnick who died in 1852 at the age of 76 and is buried in St Dunstan's churchyard. In 1909 the pond's banks burst and much of the mill was washed away. The remains, along with the miller's house, were extended to create the L-shaped black and white building glimpsed through the trees as you pass.

# Other Kent Ramblers Guides

Two of our previous guides are still available from our website or from good booksellers, both High Street and on-line.

They are:

- Guide to the Kent Coast Path Part 1: Camber to Ramsgate
- Guide to Three River Valley Walks in West Kent: Darent Valley Path, Eden Valley Walk and Medway Valley Walk

# Walks Through Time: Cranbrook South (3.6 miles)

With your back to the Information Centre turn left down Stone Street towards the windmill. At road junction keep right downhill then uphill passing the Union Windmill on the left. Take first right along Frythe Way.

At Brickenden Road turn right for a few metres then left along track between hedges (alternatively, as this path can be muddy and subject to fly-tipping, continue along Frythe Way then right along Frythe Walk to meet other end of track at turning area, shown orange on the map). On reaching street go straight ahead along the narrow Freight Lane

(restricted byway WC18A). After 700 metres or so, pass The Freight on the left (partly hidden behind Bluebell Barn) and descend to bridge. Follow edge of meadow to arable field and go straight ahead initially with hedge on left then across open field to copse and down left hand edge of field to Swattenden Lane, B2086.

Cross carefully to gap in hedge opposite. Turn left along field edge and at corner turn right uphill looking for stile or gap on left. On the other side the path should bear right through two rows of apple trees and across field to stile. However, if tree branches are obstructing the route, it may be easier to turn right to field corner then left to find stile. Over stile, go along left hand edge of next field to gap where paths cross. Turn right down middle of field to stile and bridge then along right hand side of hedge to concrete track. Take path opposite between hedges and just before corner of field take path through hedge on right. Bear right to tree and cross field to Swattenden Lane.

Turn left and follow road very carefully for 200 metres then, opposite entrance to Swattenden Adventure Centre on left, take path on right into Comfort's Wood. Bear right at first fork and right again at second, following waymarks. Cross a very small stream (dry in summer) and go through wooden kissing gate on right to leave the wood. Follow broad grassy track bearing left and taking you back to the bridge near The Freight that you crossed earlier. (As a pleasant alternative to going through the kissing gate, keep going down to river, cross and bear right uphill through Barnett's Wood to join track above The Freight – shown in orange on the map.)

Turn left and retrace your steps along Freight Lane past a double bend then take path (WC116) on left along drive. At Mount Ephraim Barn take path (WC95) on right downhill to stream. Across stream, bear left uphill, right round edge of woodland then left uphill with hedge on right. When hedge bears right, go straight ahead through two metal kissing gates to join track from former Brick Kiln Farm and turn right to High Street. Turn right down High Street back to Information Centre.

# Points of Interest

### George Hotel

Queen Elizabeth I is said to have visited the Inn in 1573 when she was given a silver gift engraved with a crown supporting the Queen's arms. The building was originally a cloth hall dating to around 1400, only part of which is now the George. It was used as a court house until the Vestry Hall was built and as a base for Customs officers pursuing smugglers in the 18th century.

Stone Street

### Old Coffee Tavern

Opposite St David's Bridge car park, built around 1890 as a temperance coffee house with reading room by Clement Cramp, a local philanthropist (1816 to 1894). Earlier this century it was Tiffins and then Raffles Restaurant but is now a private dwelling.

### The Old Bakery

The first building on the right after the car park is a 17th century timber framed building clad with red brick on the ground floor and white weather-boarding on the first floor.

### Strict Baptist Chapel

This timber framed and weather-boarded building was converted to a chapel in 1787, possibly by combining two cottages. It belongs to the Strict and Dissenting Baptists – "strict" because only those who have been baptised may

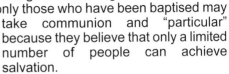
Old Coffee Tavern

take communion and "particular" because they believe that only a limited number of people can achieve salvation.

### The Old Lockup

Now Spring Cottage, just past the Chapel and on the left hand side of the road, the lock-up was built in 1850 to replace the previous lock-up which was little more than a shed and now stands in the grounds of Cranbrook Museum.

There was a room for the constable in the middle and on either side a cell without windows. It remained in use until the town's first police station was built in Waterloo Road in 1864.

## Hill House

Another timber-framed former cloth hall dating from the 15th century with later extensions and alterations. The decorative tile cladding was added in the 18th and 19th centuries. The door and early 18th century doorway deserve particular attention.

Union Windmill

## Union Windmill

This typical smock mill, although of above average height, was built in 1814. Wind being an unreliable power source for milling corn, a steam engine was installed in 1863 to drive the millstones and by 1912 the sails were so little used that they were taken down. Commercial milling ceased in 1958 and in 1960 Kent County Council acquired the mill and began restoration. There have been many cycles of refurbishment since then and the mill is fully operational for the milling of flour.

## Chapel on the Hill

The site of the former Presbyterian Chapel is marked by a plaque on the cottages on the left hand side of the road just before you turn right along Frythe Way. Apparently it occupied cottages now replaced.

## Swattenden

The mansion and surrounding buildings have been developed as an outdoor activity centre for school parties run by Adventure Kent, part of Kent County Council.

## Comfort's Wood

The Woodland Trust acquired the wood in 1990 following a donation from Dr Alex Comfort, famous as author of *The Joy of Sex*, and his wife. They were both subsequently buried in the wood and a memorial marks the spot (so they say – I didn't find it when I went looking). On acquisition the site was mainly orchard, arable and a small section of ancient woodland. In 2011 an additional area of grassland was acquired thanks to a donation from the Barnett family and this is known as Barnett's Wood. The two are managed as a single site. Planting adjacent to the ancient woodland has extended the woodland habitat and all the woodland is now being allowed to regenerate naturally. A rich diversity of wildlife has developed including 18 species of butterfly and 37 species of bird.

# The Cranbrook Colony

By the nineteenth century the Weald was no longer regarded by most outsiders as a wild and inhospitable place but was instead appreciated as picturesque and as having a landscape and society that had largely escaped the damaging effects of the industrial revolution. Those amongst the wealthy whose business interests were near enough bought large estates or smaller farms, according to their means, and developed them to enhance the impression of a rural idyll. Those whose businesses kept them far away in the midlands or north of England had to make do with works of art that represented an idealised way of life carried on in the unspoiled Wealden scenery and in houses displaying much exposed brickwork supporting bare oak beams.

"Surprise" by George Bernard O'Neill and Frederick Daniel Hardy

Amongst those catering for this market were six artists who worked together in Cranbrook and became known as the Cranbrook Colony. Frederick Daniel Hardy was the first to settle in Cranbrook, followed by Thomas Webster in 1857. Frederick's elder brother joined them as did John Callcott Horsley (designer of the world's first commercially produced Christmas card in 1843), Augustus Edwin Mulready

estlings" by George Bernard O'Neill

and George Bernard O'Neill. The six painters occupied The Old Studio which is on the left as you climb the High Street, little changed externally except that the beams are unlikely to have originally been painted so black or the infill so white. The Studio is part of a Wealden cloth hall dating from the late 15th century and now split into three cottages. Webster, who made a good income from his work, lived in an

John Callcott Horsley's first Christmas card

Surprise" by George Hardy

impressive brick house further up the High Street on the left, now called Webster House and bearing a commemorative plaque.

One of the Colony's best customers was Sidney Cartwright, a manufacturer of tin toys from Wolverhampton. He left his collection to the Wolverhampton Art Gallery which in consequence has one of the largest collections of the Colony's paintings – three of which are shown here.

# Decimus Burton

Various buildings in and around Tunbridge Wells that you pass on the routes described in this book are attributed to architect Decimus Burton.

Burton was born in London on 30 September 1800, the tenth son of builder James Burton. In 1804 the family moved to Mabledon, between Tonbridge and Tunbridge Wells, and Decimus was educated at Tonbridge School. He later spent several years at the Royal Academy Schools in Somerset House where Sir John Soane was Professor of Architecture. Decimus Burton worked initially in the office of architect John Nash who was dependent on James Burton for financing many of the buildings he designed. There he worked alongside Augustus Pugin who had come to detest the neoclassical style favoured by Soane and Nash.

Burton soon set up his own practice in London but from the late 1820s had a base in Tunbridge Wells too. Here he was commissioned to build the Calverley Estate and many country houses including Burrswood and David Salomons' Broomhill (perhaps).

His output was prolific and varied, encompassing town houses, country villas, large estates, parks and glasshouses. Buildings of particular note include the Athenaeum Club in Pall Mall, the Wellington Arch at Hyde Park Corner and the Palm House at Kew Gardens. He planned and built large estates in St Leonard's near Hastings and at Fleetwood in Lancashire.

Decimus Burton was hugely regarded in his lifetime but his legacy was diminished partly because of vicious attacks upon him by Augustus Pugin who, jealous of Burton, sought to undermine the popularity of neoclassical architecture. Pugin satirised Burton as "Talent of No Consequence, Premium Required" and John Nash as "Mr Wash, Plasterer, who jobs out Day Work on Moderate Terms". Never married, Burton retired in 1869 and died in 1881.

# Looking after the Footpaths

Although Ramblers' volunteers do much to ensure that the paths are looked after, legal responsibility rests with Kent County Council and East Sussex County Council whose budgets are much larger although still far from adequate. We have worked with both councils in preparing this book and are grateful for their support.

Path problems should be reported to the relevant council. Please feel free to report the problems to the Ramblers as well as, but not instead of, the councils.

For Kent there is an on-line reporting tool at:

https://webapps.kent.gov.uk/countrysideaccesscams/standardmap.aspx

where you can also find details of any temporary path closures. For East Sussex go to:

https://www.eastsussex.gov.uk/leisureandtourism/discover-east-sussex/rightsofway/problems-on-rights-of-way/report/.

## About the Ramblers

Most people know that the Ramblers organises led walks, enabling those who lack confidence in their navigation skills or prefer plenty of company when walking to enjoy the pleasures of walking in our wonderful countryside and towns.

Many people also know that Ramblers' volunteers work hard to ensure that our paths are protected for the enjoyment of all walkers. Some volunteers scrutinise applications to divert and close paths and ensure that the interests of walkers are protected wherever possible. If necessary they will challenge inappropriate changes to the path network at public hearings and sometimes the Ramblers will pursue cases through the courts. Other volunteers join working parties to clear vegetation that is obstructing paths and to install gates and repair stiles.

We came across quite a few problems on paths while preparing this book. There were blocked paths, waymarks that were missing or in very poor condition and even waymarks that were in completely the wrong place or directed walkers down quite the wrong path. Our volunteers have worked hard to remedy these problems where possible and in other cases we have alerted Kent County Council to deal with them, where necessary offering the funding for work using profits from the sale of our previous walking guides. Profits from this guide will also be used to improve and promote the path network.

There is always more work than we are able to do. Please support this work by joining the Ramblers, whether or not you want to walk with us, or better still become one of our volunteers.

There are so many reasons to join the Ramblers and help us to continue to create a Britain where everyone has the freedom to enjoy the outdoors on foot and benefit from the experience. Find out more about what you can do to support the Ramblers today at www.ramblers.org.uk.

Kent Ramblers' Volunteer
Recruitment Leaflet

# Acknowledgements

## General

Huge thanks are due to Colin Sefton and John Donaldson for their efforts checking out the walks in this guide and making major improvements to the waymarking of the routes.

## Mapping

Contains OS data © Crown copyright and database rights (2020).

Contains British Geological Survey materials © UKRI 2019

The base mapping is derived from Ordnance Survey data released into the public domain under the Open Government Licence. Geological maps and features are derived from BGS data released under the Open Government licence.

The footpaths in Kent and East Sussex are derived from data released by the respective county councils under the Open Government licence.

The national and regional cycle networks are reproduced by kind permission of Sustrans.

The routes of the walks are based on GPS tracks made by the author.

All other information on the maps has been created by the author.

## Photographs and Illustrations

Page 15: Photograph supplied by High Weald AONB Unit

Page 32: Photograph of Spa Valley Railway by Charlie Ralph

Page 33: Print of High Rocks by kind permission of the British Library, shelf mark K Top Vol 18

Page 35: Print of Pantiles by kind permission of the British Library, shelf mark K Top Vol 18

Page 45: Photograph of Tunbridge ware box © The Amelia

Page 53: St Dunstan, Cranbrook – Stained glass window, cc-by-sa/2.0 - © John Salmon – geograph.org.uk/p/3012368

Page 66: Goudhurst watercolour by kind permission of David Ramshaw (davidramshaw.co.uk)

Page 77: Christmas card courtesy of John Donaldson; all other images copyright: Wolverhampton Arts and Culture, www.wolverhamptonart.org.uk

All photographs and illustrations neither mentioned above nor specifically attributed where they appear are either in the public domain or are the work of the author.

Buildings on the village green, Benenden